Enjoy!

Marilyn Glick

B
Gli

Once
Upon
A
Lifetime

Marilyn's Story

Marilyn K. Glick

ONCE UPON A LIFETIME: MARILYN'S STORY

For information contact:

Hawthorne Publishing
15601 Oak Road
Carmel, Indiana 46033
317-867-5183

ISBN 978-0-9787167-5-2 Hardcover

*Our thanks to the Indianapolis Museum of Art for permission to use photographs
from their catalogue* Masters of Contemporary Glass Selections from the Glick
Collection *by Martha Drexler Lynn with Contributions by Barry Shifman copyright
1997 Indianapolis Museum of Art.*

Printed and bound in the United States of America

Dedicated to my Prince Charming,

who has given me more than any words can describe.

To him I am especially grateful for being a devoted father

to our four daughters and helping in so many beautiful and loving ways

to ease my frustrations along the way.

Today we are blessed, as the girls have blossomed and matured

into talented, caring, and special people of whom we are very proud.

It is in these young women and their growing families that

we find our greatest joy.

Table of Contents

Preface

My life is an unbelievable Cinderella story. Like Cinderella, I lost my father at an early age, and like the girl in this fairy tale, I later married a "Prince Charming," who enabled me to be the woman I am today.

In the early years I often felt different from others around me in some unknown way. It was not until I was in my twenties that I had any clue about what happened when I was born and what brought me to the only life I knew. That is a story within my story, one that is filled with surprises and revelations.

This book was intended to be very private, written for my grandchildren, great-grandchildren, and all their families who will come in future generations. I want them to know who their Grandma Bunny was and what her life was like many years ago. The world has changed so much since the time I was a girl.

I am grateful to my daughters for editing some portions of the book and for their encouragement and constructive suggestions. I could not have told this story without my editor, Nancy Baxter, who has written and edited many books about Indiana history. Nancy insisted that I should share the story beyond family members and a few friends. She believed because I had experienced important history in our city, my story would be of interest to others in this community.

For my grandchildren I started with my very first memories. Then, as I edited and re-edited, I finally understood Nancy was right, but I was determined not to delete anything I had written for my young family.

I realize that if I were a reader not acquainted with this author, I would say this story has to be fiction. Let me assure you every word is true. It all happened as I have written. While I continued to review these chapters I became more convinced than ever before that my life resembles a fairy tale. I want my very young descendants to identify with an ancestor who was once young and small perhaps like them. I hope you enjoy these recollections from the beginning to the end of this story.

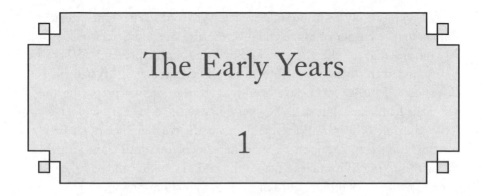

The Early Years

1

One of my earliest memories is of not wanting to go to sleep for naps. I can recall my mother rocking, rocking me, trying to get me to go to sleep. There was a picture over the mantel, a well-known one often seen in beginning art history books, Bonet's *Girl at the Fountain*.

As my mother was rocking me, she was singing a lullaby about a gypsy girl while I imagined that girl in the painting doing everything my mother's song described. Perhaps I dreamed while Mother rocked and sang. But as soon as her voice faded away, I was wide awake. All that rocking rarely put me to sleep.

Another early impression: from my crib when I was two or three—standing at the rails yelling, "I wanna get up! I wanna get up!" And sometime later, I remember tossing from side to side in my bed before going to sleep for the night while outside it was still daylight.

A few years ago while I was in California during a minor earthquake, the rolling of the bed gave me a delicious feeling of that rocking, rolling, rocking. I was disappointed when the tremors subsided because I loved the lulling sensation of rolling from side to side, so comforting. I did not want it to stop. Somewhere, somehow, in the early days of my life, there may have been a cradle and that rocking, rolling sensation, which I emulated so many times when I was a very young child waiting to fall asleep. I think I may try it out once more now in my eighth decade, when sleep does not always come easily. Today I like motion and am drawn to anything kinetic. I love to be active, to move quickly, and that must go back a long way.

I do recall my third birthday party. We lived in the upper story of a duplex on the corner of Hazelwood Street and Second Street in Detroit. My mother told me the guests would be bringing me presents. When the bell sounded from the lower foyer, I recall yelling down, "What did you bring me?" Mother must have been back in the kitchen preparing food, for if she had heard, I'm sure she would have stopped this rude query!

The only other thing I remember was the tricolor slice of ice cream, undoubtedly Neapolitan, on a glass plate: chocolate, vanilla, and strawberry. Just thinking of it makes my mouth water. I can't recall the cake—not even blowing out candles! But I'm sure that must have happened. Mother loved to bake, and she always installed an extra candle on the birthday cake, "one to grow on," she said.

I would have been about four when Mother took me for a walk in the neighborhood. A cute Boston bull terrier came up to us, a very sweet little thing. The dog seemed to like me, and I certainly was attracted to that cute pup. The terrier followed us home, and I took him out on the very long porch that went along the outside of the upper level in the front of our duplex. I lay there, playing on the floor with the dog, until suddenly this little animal began to lick my face, and I became frightened. In the meantime, my mother had read the dog tag and had already phoned the owner to come pick up his dog. I was relieved when that puppy went home.

I was a shy child, often alone. I grew up believing I was born in Detroit, Michigan, the daughter of Abraham J. and Rose Budd Koffman. In fact, I had been a nameless baby abandoned at Gouverneur Hospital in New York, where my mother died bringing me into this world. Her husband never returned to claim his child. But that story was unknown to me until I was an adult. I'll tell you about it later.

I had very few friends my age before I was six. Often I played alone in the backyard, which I truly enjoyed. I would look with wonder at the beautiful colors of the lilac bushes. Ever since that time I have loved lilacs, and although we don't have them in our yard today, we do have red bud trees, which, with their soothing color, evoke the same emotional response. Towards the back of that yard was a tree line, and in front of those trees were large clumps of decorative and delicious rhubarb. My mother would make rhubarb pies from the long, pink stems.

The only girl friend I had was Mary Lou, also an only child. I remember being in her home a few times, but I don't recall either of her parents. Mary Lou, who lived a couple of blocks away, had a handsome Airedale. She, too, was a quiet little girl. I can recall her blond hair and fair complexion, some dolls and toys, but I don't recall any conversations with her.

The other playmate I had was my doll, Lilly. I think I liked Lilly better than Mary Lou. But I don't remember any particular experiences with Lilly, either. I guess I was insecure and the best way to describe it is that I felt like a nonentity. There was a void in me that childhood play could not affect and that was not resolved until much later.

When we lived at Hazelwood and Second I loved to go over and chat with Grandma Towers, a sweet old lady who lived next door to us. She had a small wooden box with a lid on a track that slid open and closed. I loved to eat the salty codfish she always gave me from this little box. Most days I visited by going to her back door from our backyard. One day when my visit was over, she ushered me out through the front door and said, "Good-bye." I found myself alone and trapped in the foyer. I was unable to open that heavy front door leading to the outside, and it was so scary when I realized my mother didn't know where I was. Since Grandma Towers was almost deaf, she did not hear me screaming in fright. I probably screamed for five or ten minutes, but it seemed like hours. How would I ever escape?

At the time Mr. Wolfington, the owner, who lived above his tenant (Grandma Towers), was outside mowing the lawn of this beautiful, stately, gray colonial home. Finally, as he neared the front of the house, he heard me screaming. Thank the Lord, here was my savior with the magic key to free me from what I feared might be an eternal prison. Never before had I been so terrified.

Grandma Towers's daughter was single. One Saturday she took a group of us children to hear a blind pianist, providing us with a very entertaining outing that still lingers in my memory. I have always appreciated music.

Other excursions, these with my daddy, were frequent in the days before I was old enough to be in school. I loved these long, leisurely rides, just the two of us, whenever Mother was sick in bed. As we drove along country roads, passing wide open spaces, we sometimes came to a corner where a man might be standing with a pony and a sign that read "ten cents a ride." My dad thought it would be great fun for me to ride the pony. He enjoyed the break so much I never once told him how scared I was each time I was hoisted so high off the ground onto one of these animals. I was a "fraidy cat," never a "derring-do" eager for thrills.

My dad and I were often together in his big, blue Buick sedan. One day Daddy and I were driving through the city. The car door on my side had not fully locked into position when he seated me and absent-mindedly threw it shut. All went smoothly as we drove through the city, because he was unaware of the problem, until he made a left turn in heavy traffic. Suddenly the door flew open, and I found myself holding onto that door literally "for dear life." Instinctively I had grabbed the round handle on the outside of the door and was swinging on the door until he saw me and was able to stop. I enjoyed the motion and had no idea of the danger. Seat belts and car seats for small children had not even been considered in those days.

Some wonderful sounds throughout our neighborhoods are no longer heard today. My favorite was the musical tinkle coming from the Good Humor wagon that visited our area often during the summer. The melody became a familiar jingle inviting youngsters and adults to enjoy refreshing treats for ten cents each. My mouth watered as the young driver reached down into a deep freezer for a vanilla ice cream bar completely covered with a thin layer of dark chocolate. This favorite of mine, wrapped in silver foil, was called a "Frost Bite." While riding in the country, we always stopped when we spied a Good Humor truck parked along the road. Children in those days were so happy with such simple pleasures. Today I see six-year-olds who crave computer games and complicated toys, and I marvel at how sophisticated they are in our very complicated world of the twenty-first century.

Other sounds that announced delicious food were "straw-aw-berries straw—aw—aw-berries, rasss-berries—rasss-berries," sung by a vendor supporting on his shoulder a large carton with boxes of berries to sell. Probably he could not afford to rent a stall. It was simple for him to sell his produce in this way to happy customers. These berries were always so fresh and sweet.

Familiar sounds came from young newsboys, too, selling their special editions of papers "hot off the press" with spectacular news such as the kidnapping of Charles Lindbergh's baby and the crash of the Hindenburg zeppelin, for instance. The streets were filled with newsboys yelling,

"Extra, extra, read all about it." The chant went on and on for quite a while. This was the only way people could get the very latest news about important events. "Breaking news" on television was not in homes until sometime after World War II.

I should point out that most homes had radios and Victrolas, which were used to play musical records like the compact discs so popular today. When I was growing up these records were flat disks the size of dinner plates that could play everything from songs from Broadway shows to opera. There were table models and free-standing Victrola models in which you could store a lot of things in addition to stacks of records. But in the early days, these machines did not run automatically. You had to turn the handle on the side to keep the record playing, a far cry from digital televisions and iPods!

When I was five I suffered from a toothache caused by an abscessed baby tooth on the lower right side of my mouth. It needed to be extracted. I was frightened before the procedure, and my dad tried to prepare me for it. As we walked from the car to the dentist's office he sang, "In again, out again, Hooligan!" When the dentist put a gas mask over my nose, I liked the smell of the gas and was asleep in no time. Then I woke up with a heavy wad of bloody gauze where the rotted tooth had been.

The only negative thing about it was that no provision was made for the permanent tooth, which never did emerge. It is still embedded in my jaw. I was told it should be x-rayed from time to time to be sure a process of absorption was not causing damage to the roots of the teeth surrounding it. It's never been a problem.

When I was seven I had another baby tooth extracted on the upper left side. Again, no space was left for the permanent tooth. When I was in my early twenties, this tooth emerged through the roof of my mouth. Removing it was a simple procedure. All this was probably for the best, since there was certainly no room for any more teeth in my small mouth. I always felt somehow deprived as most of my friends experienced orthodontia, believing my folks had been neglectful in this area! Today I realize I was spared a lot of agony.

In these days of early childhood it was the most fun to play at Aunt Sadie's. She was my mother's sister and lived nearby. I believe she truly loved me as if I were the child she'd never had. Once she showed me a long scar from the C-section she'd had up at Saranac Lake in New York, where she had gone into labor and lost her baby.

Aunt Sadie suffered from migraine headaches, which seemed to occur frequently. After being in bed moaning and groaning most of the day, she'd baffle me by getting out of bed late in the afternoon. Then she'd spend a long time getting dressed in fine clothes to go to what I called the "sympathy." Music was the art she loved most. She knew the conductors and soloists who came to Orchestra Hall, and she became friendly with some of them, even entertaining them in her home on a few occasions. In the summer she and her husband Uncle Harry Glickman would take Mother and me to free concerts in Belle Isle Park. It was a long drive to the east side of town; we lived north and west of this park while I was growing up.

When my mother went away for the afternoon, she often left me at Aunt Sadie's. And I enjoyed being with Pearl Shipley, the housekeeper, who lived in their home as one of the family.

Aunt Sadie had taken Pearl from the "home" in Knightstown, Indiana, to do housework and take care of Beauty, an adorable fluffy white poodle who lived for twenty-three years. This was one well-cared-for pooch! The facility at Knightstown provided care and training for young people who needed a home and a way to make a living because they were not capable of learning to do skilled labor. Pearl was probably in her early teens when Aunt Sadie took her.

Pearl had lots of stories to tell and poems to recite to me. One, "Little Orphant Annie" by James Whitcomb Riley, ended several sections with "And the goblins will get YOU if you don't watch out!" She made it sound spooky!

I'm sure Pearl enjoyed having me there as much as I liked being with her, but there is one day I'll never forget. It was summer and I had a little stool on which I sat by a small patch of dirt up near the house, making mud pies. I was hot, tired, bored, and very uncomfortable. I looked around and was drawn to several cool white sheets that looked like the relief I was seeking. Years ago there was a popular song, "Doin' What Comes Naturally," and that is what I have always done, trust my instincts. Today, I do hesitate long enough to be sure no one is inconvenienced by my ever-ready instincts.

My hands were hot and sticky from the mud. I headed towards the beckoning white sheets, which Pearl had just washed and hung out to dry on the clothesline in that backyard.

It felt wonderful to wipe off all the grime and sweat on those enormous, white, cool sheets. You can be sure Pearl vented her anger on me when she saw what had happened. She must have "tanned my britches" before she pulled the dirty sheets off the line and had to wash them and then hang them up to dry again. I did not realize at the time how exasperating this must have been for her. Unfortunately it is too late to tell her I am so sorry. I certainly did not intend to make extra work for Pearl.

Christmas was a favorite time for Aunt Sadie to indulge me. We did not celebrate Christmas at my house. I received only a few Chanukah coins, called gelt, a Yiddish word for money. On Christmas Day we went to Aunt Sadie's, where she provided treasured gifts for me. One time Santa Claus left a beautiful doll wearing a deep blue velvet coat, trimmed with a white ermine collar, and a matching blue velvet beret. There was a complete wardrobe for the doll, including lace-trimmed pantaloons, which must have taken Aunt Sadie and Pearl months to sew.

Aunt Sadie and Uncle Harry truly enjoyed being with me, and Uncle Harry would take us all for a drive on Sunday to a movie, followed by dinner at Coffee Dan's downtown, where they served delicious waffles and syrup. It was a real treat.

There were many wonderful places to eat in Detroit on Sundays, but we could not go to Sanders, one of my favorites, because the owners were staunch Catholics, and they weren't ever open on Sundays. Sometimes when Mother and I shopped downtown, we would go to Sanders for lunch. We'd have an egg salad sandwich with the best mustard, made right there at Sanders. A chocolate soda at Sanders was like no other soda anywhere! It was truly delicious.

As we drove downtown on Woodward Avenue, close to the Detroit River, we would come to the Vernor's Ginger Ale sign, with little yellow lights which would bubble up like foam sparkling at the top. We'd go inside the place to enjoy a most delicious and satisfying drink. How refreshing! Vernor's on tap was so wonderful, not like anything you might drink from a bottle or can. For parties customers could rent kegs of the ginger ale. I recall the taste of it to this day.

Some summer days my parents and a group of friends would go for excursions to Put-in-Bay or Tashmoo Park. They boarded boats at the end of Woodward Avenue right on the river, and then we sailed out into Lake St. Clair. Everyone brought picnic baskets with plenty of food for lunch and dinner on the boat or on the island. There was always dancing on the boat. I recall a very tall gentleman in our group wanting to entertain me.

He asked me to dance, and that became an ordeal when I discovered, as my head rested just below his hot, sweaty waist, that he had a very offensive body odor. I would have liked to have held my breath, but I simply had to get some air or suffocate. I was just miserable until that dance was over and I was back with my parents and breathing normally.

Aunt Sadie and Uncle Harry belonged to the Beth-El Reform Temple in Detroit, located one block from our home. When I started Sunday school, I went to Beth-El. Even though it was only one block away, my dad would drive me there and pick me up when it was over. I really hated that because Daddy was usually late. The classroom was up on the second floor and I waited for him there. It was really awful because the teacher did not stay with us. As my classmates left one at a time, I would become aware that I was the only one left. I feared Daddy would never come for me, and I was scared, crying until he finally arrived. Eventually I found out I could go downstairs into the sanctuary where others waited. After that I was never alone until Daddy came to take me home.

My parents belonged to the Conservation congregation and were very observant. We did not ride on Shabbos, nor spend money on Shabbos. More Orthodox relatives, like the Sachses and the Dushkins, did not even write, turn on electricity, or light a fire for heating or cooking. The Sachses were my father's sister Aunt Fannie and her husband, Uncle Ed. Their daughter was Helen Dushkin and her husband was Max. Helen and Max had three children: Mike the oldest; Sonia, my age; and the youngest, Faye, a few years younger than I. These children were not even allowed to play cards on Shabbos, which was truly a day of rest, not much fun. The older men were supposed to study the holy books on this day. My folks went to services every Saturday. I did not enjoy that when I was young and did not go to the synagogue with them. My time devoted to synagogue would come later.

Mother always loved little ones and didn't want to part with me, so she decided to keep me home from kindergarten when other children my age were beginning public school. Complicating the matter was a medical condition doctors diagnosed as "acidosis." In those days a lot of emphasis was placed on children eating well: it was a mark of plenty in the home as well as that of a healthy child. She urged food on me; and often although I didn't want it, I ate to please her. My overloaded stomach began to give me trouble. I don't know if this contributed to her keeping me home in 1927 or if it was just that she wanted to have her baby close to her a while longer.

I was five years old in March of 1927, and I should have started kindergarten in the fall of that year. It was not until late January, 1928, that I was finally allowed to enter school. What an interesting and pleasurable new world this kindergarten class offered, with so many other children and a motherly teacher guiding and befriending us!

I achieved one of my heart's desires in that half year of kindergarten. More than anything else in the world I wanted "Ima Walker." This was a doll on a stick popular with quite a few of the other girls, who sometimes brought the doll to school with them. It was a clever, inexpensive toy made of two heavy cardboard pieces shaped like a little girl, on which the face was painted with long, dark curly hair. Ima's dress was an attractive lavender print. In between the two skirts back and front was a round disk from which hung pairs of black Mary Jane shoes over white anklets. The little shoes rotated on a disk, which made the doll appear to walk. This marvelous toy was propelled with a long, smooth wooden stick attached just below the shoulders at the back.

I came out of school one day and saw my mother waiting for me with an Ima Walker. You can't imagine how thrilled I was. I marvel at how much our minds are like today's computers. I have not thought about Ima Walker since we left Hazelwood and Second. Yet it was saved in vivid detail on my inner hard drive. We tend to save whatever is important to us. The rest goes into the trash bin. I believe that begging for Ima Walker taught me persistence, and I also discovered that it is all right to ask for what you want and believe you need.

When I was almost five and a half, we moved from Hazelwood and Second into a brand new apartment building. We were on the first floor of a three-story building called the Maravilla, right on the corner of Chicago Boulevard and Wildemere Street. And I loved everything about the Maravilla.

My parents had driven around for over a year looking for more up-to-date living quarters, as my father's real estate business prospered with the boom going on in the late 1920s. They considered only homes or apartments that were newly built. Finally they chose the Maravilla, shortly before the building was completed. We moved in the late summer of 1928. That building had a social room, and our first-floor unit had the only porch in the facility. I loved to watch the logs glowing in the gas fireplace in the living room.

The year 1928 marked major changes in my young life. Not only did we move to the Maravilla, but I also entered first grade at Brady School. I had had only one semester of kindergarten, but now I began learning some basic reading skills with simple words and sentences.

I began attending the Sunday school at the Conservative synagogue, Shaarey Zedeck, and came to like those classes. I was learning Jewish history from the Bible stories, and I made quite a few friends at Sunday school too. Many of these girls were also in my classes in public school, and their parents knew my parents, so we were friends growing up together. Some of those friends I have kept in touch with throughout our adult years.

In January, when most youngsters in my class were advancing to the second half of first grade, Mother discovered an old friend who lived in a building on Chicago Boulevard, across the street and just several buildings further down the block. This friend, Mrs. Wolf, had a daughter, Lorraine, who was ready for the first semester of second grade at that time. Mother learned her friend's daughter was only one month older than I. Lorraine Wolf was a big girl (somewhat overweight). We called her "Lorrie Wobbles." My birthday was in March; Lorraine was born in February.

Lorraine had no doubt started kindergarten in the fall of 1927. When the semester changed in January 1928, because Lorraine was big for her age and because she was only a few weeks shy of her sixth birthday, she was advanced to first grade at the time I was just beginning kindergarten. So in the fall of 1928, as I enrolled at my new school, I was placed in the first semester of first grade, while Lorraine progressed with her class into the second semester of first grade.

When Mother realized I was one-half semester behind Lorraine, she arranged for me to advance to second grade with her, after I had completed only the first semester of first grade. I was placed in second grade without having a sufficient introduction to reading and writing.

I remember sitting next to a girl named Marjorie on the first day of second grade. I was confused and not sure what to do. However, I was able to see and copy the first three letters of my name from Marjorie's paper. On the reading test that day we both got the miserable score of three identical correct answers out of twenty-four. I had copied everything from Marjorie's test. What else could I have done?

I was on probation for the first six weeks and almost failed. Until I caught on to reading a little better, I had a great deal of difficulty with spelling tests. It was only in the sixth week that I finally managed to get an acceptable grade and was able to stay in the second grade class. My first grade of 100% on a spelling test was a big thrill! Later, when I was eight years old, an eye test at school revealed I needed glasses, which helped considerably with reading. For many years, I had difficulty reading out loud in front of the class. To this day, I am a slow reader.

Throughout these early years we always lived close enough to the school for me to walk home for lunch each day. That was healthful, though sometimes it presented special challenges. In the new neighborhood there were apartments all along Chicago Boulevard, but except for the buildings on the corner facing Chicago, Wildemere was a street of single-family homes. The direct walk from school to the Maravilla led me home on Wildemere past a house guarded by a threatening German shepherd, whose bark really scared me! Each time I walked by with a pounding heart, I held my breath and pretended not to see that menacing dog.

At school I met Marilyn Watson, who frequently walked part way home with me in the afternoon. She lived some long blocks past my apartment. I believe her parents were divorced. Anyway, one day a friend of hers walked home with me instead. I don't know if she had been put up to it or not, but the friend made some derogatory remarks about Marilyn. And I agreed, perhaps adding some negative words as well. After the friend went back to Marilyn and reported what I had said, Marilyn was very mad at me. The next day she hit me and made me cry. That was when I learned the lesson, "If you don't have something nice to say about someone, don't say anything at all." We made up subsequently, and I have some vague remembrance that my mother called her mother and patched things up for me.

The first year we lived in the Maravilla, to celebrate my seventh birthday my mother had a big party in the social room, entertaining twenty-five children. Among the presents these girls brought to the party were three beautiful dressy handbags. Although I was thrilled to get them, I didn't need so many fancy party bags. Mother took them downtown to the J. L. Hudson department store and exchanged them for cash. Then we went to a wholesale house and she bought me a large, red raincoat; a blue sweater; and another wholesale bargain, much more practical. I had that raincoat until I outgrew it when I was twelve years old. I would have preferred that she had let me keep the purses!

That one blue sweater was a part of my wardrobe for years. I turned the sleeves up a lot at first, then gradually let them down until I was perhaps in my early teens. Even when my mother could afford to be extravagant, she was extremely frugal. When she entered a grocery store, she would head for the quick-sale produce table to pinch each orange so she could get the best ones on sale. I thought I had inherited her passion for bargains. I would go downtown before the stores opened on sale day and always I'd bring home wonderful buys. I particularly recall a truly beautiful blue wool coat our first-born Marianne had when she was a tiny girl. Gene used to tease me by saying that when the department store sales clerks saw me, they would say, "There's Mrs. Glick! Bring out the half-price tickets." But that was years in the future.

When I was eight, Mother tried to teach me to play the piano, but it didn't work out well. Mother didn't have much patience with me in that endeavor, so she gave up. A few years later she got me a professional piano teacher, a woman who taught rigidly. As the other children were out playing, I was inside going over scales and finger exercises, practicing an hour a day. Only twenty minutes of that time could be spent on playing a piece; the rest of the time was spent on scales and finger exercises. There was no joy in all this practice.

I couldn't really see the half and quarter notes very well and that slowed me down. I think my eyes weren't good at the time. Still, I wish I'd had more interesting piano selections to play. The instrument I played on was a fine one. My father and mother had just purchased a new Wurlitzer baby grand piano. Three or four times a year the extended family got together, and the other little girls: my cousins Sonia, Marcia, and Eileen, would play nice little piano pieces, melodies by Chopin or Mozart, and I would have to play this simple little piece, "On the Ice at Sweet Briar," by some unknown composer. I was miserable on these occasions.

Incidentally, in 1960, when Gene and I moved into our new home, Mother let me have her beautifully carved treasure of a piano for the new house. My interior designer, Mr. Al Samuels, who designed and remodeled furniture in a large facility he had on Twenty-second, between Illinois Street and Capitol Avenue, admired the piano. He had come to the U.S. from Germany during the Holocaust, and his background included the fine arts. Though I do not play it any more, I love having this piano in our living room. When they were young, my three oldest daughters took some lessons on the piano. But there were so many other things they preferred to do that they didn't have much interest. A few years ago Arlene bought her own baby grand piano and enjoyed taking lessons and practicing.

In those days at the Maravilla, I was troubled by warts on the calves of my legs. My uncle in Indianapolis, Dr. Witt, recommended some liquid we would apply with a small wooden stick. This usually helped to dry them up. But I had one on the outside of my right arm just below the elbow that would not go away. Because it was in a vulnerable spot, I kept bumping it, and it got to be all colors, including brown and sometimes shades of purple.

Finally my folks had a doctor in Detroit look at it, and he advised them to have it removed. I was seven or eight at that time. I was on the operating table for twenty-five minutes (local anesthetic), and the nurses kept bragging about how brave I was. Apparently, it was much deeper than they had anticipated. I left the hospital having experienced no memorable pain, and I liked the sling they put on my arm. But when I got home that day, I discarded the sling and with the bandaged right arm played jacks, one of my favorite games, with my friends. The scar was prominent for a while, but I never think of it or notice it now.

There were interesting friends in that Maravilla apartment building. Bobby Lipson would come to stay with his grandmother, Jennie Lipson, a good friend of my folks. Jennie Lipson had moved into this building in 1928 when we came to live there and occupied an apartment identical to ours on the third floor. A few months later her husband died while he was in New York on business.

Bobby was close to three years younger than I, but we had wonderful afternoons playing cards. We always played War with enormous stacks of Jennie's overused bridge cards. About 4 p.m. Jennie would fix us hot chocolate and cookies. She was an elegant lady, tall and stately, who had had snow-white hair from an early age; she once told us she washed her hair at home and used bluing in the rinse water. Some years later Jenny moved to Chicago, and my mother corresponded with her for many years.

Jenny's son, Bernie Lipson, the father of Bobbie, was married to Estelle, this stunning fashion plate of a woman with a wonderful personality, Bobbie's mother. Some few years after Bobbie and I played War at the Maravilla, Bernie and his wife were divorced; and Estelle married my cousin, Dave Schiller. Dave was one of Aunt Anna Schiller's sons, and his first wife was Dorothy Schnabel. Bernie and Estelle had been close friends with Dave and Dorothy. As sometimes happens, my cousin fell in love with Estelle, Bernie's wife, and both Dave and Estelle divorced their original spouses to marry each other. They spent the rest of their lives very happily together. From time to time Gene and I see the grown-up Bobbie Lipson and his wife, Shirley, when we are in Florida. When we celebrated our fiftieth wedding anniversary, they came to Indianapolis for our big party at the Indianapolis Museum of Art.

At Brady School one of the mothers in the school would come to school and take pictures of the children in our class. I loved the photos she gave to all of us. A few years later her son Eliot was in line with me and he pulled my hair. I couldn't make him stop, so I went to the teacher and told on him, getting him into a lot of trouble. I felt quite guilty about reporting this boy whose mother had been so kind to me and the rest of the class.

I recall a particular incident when I first got my first taste of fund-raising. One Sunday in early May when I was seven, Daddy brought me a little blue canister with a metal top and a slot for coins. He asked if I would like to collect money for Jewish National Fund Flower Day. I was to express thanks to each contributor and hand out a lovely little pale blue daisy with a white center on a slender wire stem, wrapped in soft grass-green raffia to resemble a real flower. The petals matched the canister.

The mission of the JNF was to plant trees in Palestine, the land that was to become the state of Israel after World War II. I was excited—it would be fun and rewarding. First I knocked on the door of everyone living in the Maravilla. Of course they would not refuse.

After our lunch, my dad went out to collect rents. Friends of my mother had invited her to drive with them to Mt. Clemens, and they were happy to have me come along with my wares. Mt. Clemens was a spa community a short distance outside the city of Detroit, with a small number of hotels catering to arthritic elderly people. These people had come to Mt. Clemens to take advantage of the therapeutic mineral baths, and on Sunday afternoon the hotel guests were all sitting out in front of their hotels in rocking chairs. In no time, my canister was filled. The next week the De- troit *Jewish Chronicle* published a photo of me holding the canister and the daisy accompanied by a story recounting how I had collected more money that day than any other volunteer. I have enjoyed fund-rasing ever since.

Inspired by this success, I wanted to collect more money, but this time for myself. I founded the Rainbow Club, dues a penny a year. I had no trouble enrolling a membership of 33 friendly Maravilla residents at such a nominal fee. I listed the paid members of the club in a slender little notebook. But we would never meet, because this was a club for me alone. It was going to be great, but greed got the better of me. Daddy had a chiforobe (tall chest of drawers) in his bedroom, where I noticed he placed loose change in a small drawer at the top. When my folks were away from the apartment, I would climb up on a stool and remove all the pennies I could find. After a while, Daddy mentioned the theft to my mother. I was caught and they made me return every one of the pennies to the members of my club and perhaps the bulk of this money to my dad. Thus the Rainbow Club completely collapsed but I learned a vital lesson: "Thou shalt not steal," as God commanded.

My mother had what could be described as a neurotic personality. When I was a small girl and my family lived at Hazelwood and Second, Mother was prone to fainting and taking to her bed for days. But at no time while we lived in the Maravilla do I recall Mother having one of her "spells." She and I were getting along very well. I remember in second grade I had to write a short paper and she composed it for me:

I am a robin
I have a beautiful red breast
I like to get worms for my babies
Best of all I like to sing.

Perhaps the security of the situation helped her.

For the most part, I was a "goody goody" child, but there were a number of times I was not really so good. Once I was playing in the backyard of the Maravilla and broke a basement window. I can't recall whether I threw a ball or ran into that window with my tricycle. I didn't own up to it, and don't know if anyone ever knew I was responsible. Another time, Lorraine Wolf became friends with some girls who were just a little older. We must have been about eight. They were smoking cigarettes in the basements of their apartment buildings. Perhaps because they needed another place to smoke, they drafted me to participate. At least I went with them to smoke in the basement of the Maravilla.

No one seemed to see us, and I really did not feel guilty about it. But I was out front one evening and a family friend, Harry Greenberg, who lived in the building, whispered in my ear, "Do you smoke?" My heart pounded as I told him no. Possibly his housekeeper had observed us while she was washing their clothes in the basement laundry room. That was the end of my smoking with those girls.

Our family seemed pleased and proud to be living in the Maravilla apartment. My dad had invested equity in properties and collected rents that more than covered the many mortgage payments, leaving us with plenty of money to enjoy an upscale lifestyle. We did live well at the beautiful Maravilla.

My dad figured his net worth one night and realized that he was worth a quarter of a million dollars. In those days, this was truly a substantial accomplishment. That was August of 1929.

Then the stock market crashed, in October of that year.

The banks declared a holiday, and people who had money deposited in the banks were unable to get it out. Most had invested heavily in the market because it seemed everyone was making it big and that was the way to go. No one in our family had much money after that! The exceptions were Lil and Dave Diamond. Lil was my Aunt Anna Schiller's oldest daughter. Her husband Dave, owner of the Diamond Screw Works, had made a fortune during World War I.

My father had made a mistake investing so heavily in the stock market. He and a wealthier man who was a member of his extended family but not closely related, had invested together, buying stocks in tandem. His name was Oscar Schiller, and he was my Uncle Joe Schiller's cousin.

Oscar was out of town when it became obvious that the boom in stocks was over—the bubble was about to burst, 1929. My dad realized they needed to sell their stocks, but didn't feel he could do so without consulting Oscar, who was out of town. Communications in that day were not the easy thing they are today, with e-mail, faxes, and cell phones producing immediate answers to vital questions. He waited a few days until Oscar got back to Detroit, but by the time his partner returned, my dad was pretty well wiped out. He had tried to be considerate and not act alone. Too bad!

Some things changed. With no income from the tenants in his real estate properties, there was not enough money to make all the mortgage payments. We could no longer afford the rent we had been paying at the Maravilla, so we had to move to less expensive quarters—to another apartment, this one about a mile away on Richton Avenue. I also attended a new school where I made new friends.

At the time of the crash Daddy was the treasurer of the B'nai B'rith. The organization's bank account was ruined, too, and even though he had lost most of his money, my father felt responsible. Daddy provided his own funds to pay off all their debts. My father was an ardent Zionist, and he put his heart into that cause, even buying a forest of trees in what became the state of Israel years later.

Typical of the type of generosity and concern for others Daddy displayed was what he did for a man who was "consumptive," suffering from tuberculosis, a Mr. Brussels. This man had a dozen children and was poor as a church mouse. Whenever Mr. Brussels came around during the Depression to see us, my father would empty his pockets and give the man whatever he had. Gene's beloved grandfather, Adolph Biccard, was the same sort of man, and Gene learned early to be generous in helping others. Years later, that was one of the things that attracted me to Gene; he had many of the good qualities I'd come to value in my father.

One mortgage company after another foreclosed on Daddy's properties, so his business was drying up. My father decided to become an insurance agent for Travelers Insurance Company, one of the leading insurance companies in the Detroit area. He sold a million dollars worth of life insurance the first year, so in August of 1932 he won an all-expenses-paid trip to the Château Frontenac in Montreal. If Mother was to accompany him, he would have had to pay for her to go.

"I don't want to leave Marilyn," she said, but I think she didn't want to spend the money. What a shame! I would have liked having her go, because I would have gone over to the house of my cousins, Sonia and Faye Dushkin, and had a good time. I came to believe Mother should have gone with him. He would have enjoyed having her with him.

Richton was not very far from the old neighborhood, but now I attended Roosevelt, which was the elementary school building in the center of the campus between Durfree Intermediate (grades 7-9) and Central High School (grades 10-12). Playgrounds, tennis courts, and baseball fields were closest to the street. The school buildings were set further back covering a wide area. My walk to school was about a half mile each way.

A friend from Sunday school during this period was June Smith, although we were not close. I really did not have close friends until I was about twelve. My mother played bridge with June's mother, and I was always invited to June's birthday parties. June and I spent many long summer afternoons together.

I spent more time with Rosalie Frank than I did with June. Rosalie and I met when we were in the same fourth grade Sunday school class at Shaarey Zedeck. Later we were in some of the same classes at Durfee Intermediate and Central. Our friendship developed further in a few years.

I was a good student who worked hard at school. One of the lessons we learned was that World War I had been the war to end all wars. How happy I was to be living at a time when the world was civilized. Our generation would be immune from the horrors we read about in our history books, my world safe and secure. So it seemed.

When I was very young, people would ask me, "Who do you like better, your mother or your father?" I think that was a question that was asked then, though it seems odd to me now. I would say "I like them both the same." For me it was the truth as I saw it, but my answer may have stemmed from more complicated feelings.

When my mother had her spells and was confined to bed for a long time, Daddy would take me with him for rides in the Buick four-door sedan. One time my father told me, "When people ask you who do you like best, you should say, 'I like my mother best.'" He probably thought it would make her happy. So I did as he instructed and in time I came to believe it. It wasn't until I was ten years old, when some heart problems put Daddy in the hospital in Ann Arbor, to be followed by three weeks of recuperation, that I really began to look at things differently. I began to sense then how much I loved him.

The last time I saw my daddy was before sundown on April 11, 1933, close to the end of the first day of Passover. We were spending the holiday week with my dad's sister Anna Schiller. The Schillers lived in the upper half of a duplex on Pingree near Linwood. I was playing checkers with Milton Sheyer, the husband of Aunt Anna's youngest daughter Ruthie. The Sheyers lived in Saginaw and had driven in to celebrate the second Seder with the family.

When I am concentrating on a game, I am totally enrapt in planning my strategy and almost oblivious to whatever else is going on about me. I'm still that way! I was aware of Daddy's leaving, and by the time he had reached the foyer downstairs, a thought flashed through my mind, "Suppose he doesn't come back." Ever since I had realized he had a heart problem, I always kissed him goodbye when he left the house. I wish I had called down, had him wait for my goodbye kiss. But I did not interrupt my checkers game, and he walked on to Shaarey Zedeck, at the corner of Chicago Boulevard and Lawton Street.

When he reached the synagogue, they said he sat next to a doctor. Daddy said, "It's getting dark in here." And then he was gone forever. Daddy, Daddy, Daddy, how I cried and how I missed him.

There were thirty-three of us waiting for Daddy to come back from the services. Carl Schiller, Anna's oldest son, finally returned from the synagogue and announced, "Uncle Abe is in heaven." A few days later, the funeral was held in the crowded living room of the Schiller home. I will never forget the moment toward the end of the service when they sang the final song, *El Male Rachamim.* Then they closed the casket—the end of the life I held most dear.

Up to that time, I had not thought much about myself as a person. Inside I had always felt like a nonentity, but now I had to think of who I was and what I was. I looked to God and to my Daddy in heaven. I wanted to be good, and I wanted Daddy to be proud of me, to please him more than anything in the world. And because my dad was well known in the Jewish community, people would be watching me. Whatever I did would be a reflection on his reputation, and it was important for people to think highly of me for his sake. I never said this to anyone, but this is how I felt inside.

I learned another thing that I had never before realized. No one is immune to adversity. Before this time I would read in the newspapers or hear from family or on the radio of terrible things happening to people. I always thought of this as happening to others. Now I realized how much like our fellow human beings we all are.

Religion was now very important to me, and I practiced all our rites and traditions with zeal and conviction. We kept the kosher dietary laws, for instance, and I didn't ride on the Sabbath. My friends wanted to pick me up to go to the movies but I said no. Today I realize how my faith and observance sustained me during this time of great need.

I loved Sunday school and excelled there. I went to the Junior Congregation at Shaarey Zedeck and became a very active member, attending all their services on the Sabbath and holidays. Twice a year the Junior Congregation had the privilege of conducting services in the main synagogue. I was honored at least three or four times to be asked to speak before the large congregation to explain the sedra, part of the Torah that was being read that Saturday. I worked hard on preparing these speeches and loved the glory of performing before such a large group of grown ups.

All of us young people were within two or three years of each other in age, and we grew up together. Not only was it an opportunity for me to participate religiously, but it was a social experience. I liked to be in a leadership position. Could that be innate?

When I spoke before the adult congregation, I had butterflies in my stomach, but that only helped me do a better job. Without being so keyed up, the talk might have been a big flop. Anyway, I received the compliments I was seeking, my mother was proud, and I felt Daddy was looking down on me and was pleased.

On special holidays, four times a year, there is a Yiskor, or memorial service recited by those who have lost loved ones. It was a time for me to let the world know how I loved and missed my daddy. I cried long and loud. I wanted these people to know how I felt, and today I believe this was therapeutic for me as well. On occasions when older people who were long-time family friends died or were perhaps killed in some accident, I would take their deaths very hard and would lie in bed, truly ill, just trying to cope with the event.

So my daddy's death caused me not only pain and grief, but resulted in my extremely strong ties to Shaarey Zedeck, Judaism, and the charitable causes that had been so dear to my father. Later his memory caused me to be determined to marry a man like him with high moral values, a strong love of humanity, and a caring and generous nature.

After our first daughter Marianne was born, I felt the presence of my dad standing on the other side of my hospital room, the only vision I had of him since he died. I never again felt his presence. I guess he was satisfied with the life I was leading; I hope so. I loved him dearly. When he died, my childhood ended. And for years I was alone with my mother.

My first birthday party with my dad and mother and (l–r) Marcia Diamond, Eileen Schiller, Henry Erlich, Mike Dushkin, Marilyn, and Sonia Dushkin. There's an extra candle on the cake "to grow on."

Grandma Towers, who lived next door, was a good friend.

Guess who!

Hazelwood and Second, my first home in Detroit. We lived upstairs. Grandma Towers lived in the first house to the right.

*A. J. and
Rose Koffman
waited fifteen
years before I
joined them.*

*My doll Lilly and I enjoy
a moment in the snow.*

My mother, her brother Jake Budd, Harry and Sadie Glickman and I. My dad is peeking over Jake's shoulder.

On the sidewalk in front of our apartment on Richton. Our family auto is across the street.

Aunt Sadie and Uncle Harry moved to Detroit when he accepted a position as head of tailoring at a downtown department store.

Rose (l) and Sadie were sisters, and some Budd family resemblance is obvious in these engagement portrait photos from the first decade of the twentieth century.

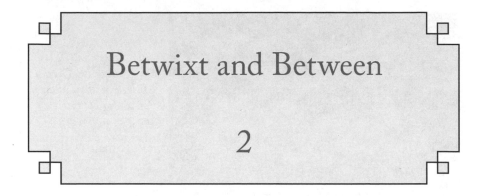

Betwixt and Between

2

My mother, Rose Budd, grew up in Indianapolis. Her father died at age forty, when she was only six, and that must have influenced her life, as it did mine. She had a younger sister with whom she was very close, but this sister, Rachel, caught pneumonia along with their father, and she died too. My mother was next youngest, then Aunt Sadie, who was six years older. Jake (J. E. Budd), her brother, was fourteen at the time his father and sister died, and Anna was the oldest child in the family. So it was Anna, Jake, Sadie, Rose, and Rachel.

It is interesting to note how many immigrants assumed new names when they came to America. My mother's father and his family were happy and thrilled to land in this country, and they loved the boat that had brought them here. So they adopted the name of the boat, the *Budweitsky*. Many years later I learned the family's name was really Levin and some of their relatives had settled in Des Moines, Iowa.

Uncle Jake changed the name Budweitsky to Budd, and since Mother was named Rose, she became a Rose Budd! My mother was born in Indianapolis in 1884. If she were living today, she'd be 123.

My maternal grandparents were Casper and Mary Budweitsky. Casper came from Poland originally and Mary from Germany. I have no idea how they met and married, nor how they happened to settle in Indianapolis. My grandmother had a brother, Isador Fierst, who lived in Zanesville, Ohio, and I met him, but just once.

My mother's family lived on south Capitol Avenue, a block or two south of the area where Shapiro's Delicatessen is today. Their house of prayer was Shaarey Tefilla, an Orthodox congregation

Casper, like many other immigrants with large families to support, became a peddler. Many of these immigrant men had horse-drawn carts which were used to travel through alleys to pick up scrap materials that could be used to make goods to earn money.

Some men in the neighborhood picked up scrap metal and eventually developed lucrative steel businesses. Casper picked up paper and made wipers to dust desks in offices of large businesses throughout the city. Jake Budd took over the company at the age of fourteen, after his father died, building it into a prosperous enterprise. J. E. Budd Company stood for years at 501 South Capitol, on the site of the present modern U.S. post office administration building.

Jake married Kate Bluestein from Cincinnati, Ohio. One of Kate's cousins became the movie actress known as Joan Blondell. Jake and Kate Budd had three sons: Clarence, the oldest; then Harold; and finally the youngest, Lester. Lester, who was seventeen years older than I, was quite handsome and very sweet. It was Lester who nicknamed me "Poozie," a nickname only he and his brothers ever used.

Once each summer when I was a child, my family would drive to Indianapolis for our annual "vacation." To be close to my mother's sister Annie Witt, who lived a short walk from the south end of downtown, we stayed in a small hotel, either the Lockerbie or the Spencer House across from Union Station. It was on these trips that I got to know my Budd relatives, Mother's family.

Lester Budd was the cousin I loved most, certainly the one bright light on these trips to Indianapolis. We would sit for hours just talking on the porch at Aunt Annie's house.

Annie was my mother's oldest sister. When her father died, she had just graduated from high school and was a tall, attractive young woman. She was also an accomplished piano teacher. About this time Lazarus Witt came to Indianapolis, after having migrated to America following his education in Russia as a physician. However, when he arrived in America, it was necessary for him to have a degree from a university in the U.S. to practice medicine here, so he enrolled at Johns Hopkins, the leading medical school in the United States at that time.

When he came out of that school, this highly educated young man was ready to set up his practice, and he decided to "Go West." Arriving in Indianapolis, he was considered a "good catch" by the small Jewish community living on the south side. It was almost inevitable that he should meet the beautiful and talented Anna Budweitsky, and they could not help but fall in love and marry.

Dr. Witt's office was the converted dining room of his house. Though he had a fine medical practice, with patients coming from all sides of town, not just the south side, he turned out to be eccentric, quite strange really. In later life Annie developed colitis, and he gave her strict instructions about what to eat, for instance to take her chicken off the bones and cut and eat it in tiny pieces. She used syringes every day and really was ill.

When I knew her, my Aunt Annie Witt had become a fragile and pathetic old woman, pale, very thin, with short straight white hair, wearing no makeup and always clad in a gingham house dress. Our visits may have been the only break she ever experienced in the monotony of a painful, humble existence.

Lazarus Witt owned a double house on south Illinois Street, just north of Shapiro's Delicatessen, and it was in this double that the family lived. The Witt house is still there. The Witts' son Clarence was very bright and could also play the piano well. Clarence had seizures, possibly epilepsy, when he was very young, so his doctor father would never let him go out when he was older. He didn't want Clarence to marry and pass on what may have been a genetic predisposition to epilepsy, so he wasn't allowed to be with other boys and girls or eventually date. Possibly the seizure problem was in the Witt family; nobody in the Budd family had this problem.

Clarence stayed in that home, playing the piano, never seeing a movie or going anywhere. He read extensively, books on religion and philosophy throughout the ages. He also studied the stock market and must have advised his dad on their stock investments, where I believe Lazarus Witt had put most of his money. The Witts spent almost nothing, never traveling or going out to dinner, movies, or concerts.

Anyway, my mother and I would sit on Aunt Annie's porch, visiting with the family on those summer mornings, and it was really boring. I suffered patiently until Lester came to rescue me at noon. He would take me to Shapiro's (still located on South Meridian Street today), and after lunch we would walk to the J. E. Budd and Company office. There I spent a happy afternoon pounding on their old Underwood typewriter until the office closed at 5 p.m. For a number of years after my dad died, Lester and I corresponded. He sent me presents. I remember just one—a beige leather pocketbook. After Daddy died, we would drive to Indianapolis with Aunt Sadie and Uncle Harry, the aunt and uncle whose house and companionship I loved as a young child.

I don't have much knowledge of Sadie's early years. She must have finished eighth grade before she went to work in downtown Indianapolis. Her husband, Uncle Harry Glickman, had come to Indianapolis from Albany, New York, having evidently emigrated from Russia earlier. There were many pogroms and reasons for Jews to leave Russia at the end of the nineteenth century.

A friend had come to Indianapolis with him. When Harry was dating Sadie, my mother got to know Harry's friend and was attracted to him. She fell in love with this young man, but did not feel she could marry him. He had a terrible temper, and my mother was a practical person. She really was afraid that he might abuse her, and she didn't want to take that risk. I think this young fellow was the man she loved. I had come to believe she married my dad for security, not for love.

As a girl Mother went to the local south side schools in Indianapolis. Her family did not have much money after their father died, and she had to quit school after the third grade. She walked north to the center of town, where she worked each day in a millinery shop. She was a good salesgirl and learned how to embellish the hats to satisfy the whims of her wealthy customers. Later this very bright young girl educated herself reading novels. Most of all she enjoyed Honore Balzac, Gustave Flaubert, Victor Hugo, Mark Twain, Booth Tarkington, and other well-known writers.

My grandmother, Mary Budd, whom I called "Little Grandma," was very religious. She was quite elderly when I knew her, and I adored her. Little Grandma Budd came up to Detroit to stay with me when my father was ill the first time with heart trouble. Daddy was admitted to the hospital in Ann Arbor on the campus of the University of Michigan, and I came to know Little Grandma Budd well during that time. She was a darling. I played Casino with her for hours, and she told me stories about Jesus being excommunicated from the synagogue because he claimed that he had supernatural powers. When there was a thunderstorm, she would walk up and down in our apartment carrying her prayer book and reading prayers, one for thunder and another for lightning. Grandma Budd died at age eighty-four, when I was twelve.

My father, Abraham Jacob Koffman, came to this country when he was four years old. His father's family had many brothers and sisters who came at the same time, settling throughout Michigan, with many of them living in Detroit. I thought I was related to half the Jewish community in Detroit.

My father was the youngest in his immediate family. When they arrived from Russia at Ellis Island, the officials spelled the family name Koffman. It is an odd, uncharacteristic spelling.

There is an interesting sidelight connected with that spelling of the name. Within the last ten years, I read that Mervyn Manning from Detroit had joined our club in Florida. I was not familiar with that name, and none of the Detroit friends I queried knew them either. Later I learned that Mervyn had been an executive with Ford Motor Company. This interesting couple had lived in France, Asia, and elsewhere, not spending much time in Detroit.

I wondered about them. At dinner one night in Boca Raton, I asked a more recent Detroit friend, Marilyn Gordon, about them and she told me, "Yes, I know them. Elaine Manning, the woman you're asking about, is my cousin." "What was her maiden name?" I wanted to know. After fewer than twenty questions, I learned that Elaine's father was Al Koffman the druggist, who was my father's first cousin. It was quite a surprise that Elaine Manning's grandfather was my grandfather's brother! I could hardly wait to get in touch with these Koffman cousins. Now we have become good friends in Florida.

My Grandpa Koffman had lost his first wife some years after my parents were married. On the night of the first Passover Seder each year, we went to Grandpa's house, where his second wife Brini had spent countless hours preparing for the Passover and this traditional Seder feast. In one portion of the Seder service the leader hides the afikomin, half of one of three sheets of matzo (unleavened bread) placed on a Seder plate, all wrapped in large white napkins. The child who finds this hidden afikomin receives a present. When there are many children participating in the hunt, this is fun, but here I was with my mom and dad and two very elderly grandparents. So it was not very exciting, and to make the game even less exciting I always knew what the prize would be. The only gift Grandpa ever gave me was the same every year, a pink silk one-piece undergarment, which I never wore!

Hyman Koffman was an old man when I knew him, and I was uncomfortable when my parents took him for a ride in our car. He seemed to have some respiratory problem that made him cough and spit, so I wasn't attracted to him as a child. I hate to say it, but I found him repulsive then.

I know very little about my father's childhood and youth growing up in Detroit. As a youngster he was called Abe, and later he was known as A. J. He never spoke about his service in World War I, but I saw pictures of him as a young man in uniform. Vaguely I sense there was a broken engagement to another girl some time before he met my mother.

His wife-to-be, my mother, had grown up, as I've said, three hundred miles away, down south in Indiana with the Budd family. All of the Budd offspring were tall and handsome, and my mother was particularly beautiful. That was to play a part in how they met.

Mother's aunt, who lived in Detroit, was Bailey Smith, my grandmother's sister, whose husband was a shamos, the sexton, of the Orthodox synagogue in a neighborhood where the early Jewish settlers lived in Detroit. Abe Koffman's mother was a friend of Bailey Smith and often went to visit her. A recent photograph of Rose Budd, obviously a beautiful young woman, was on a table in the living room.

One afternoon Abe stopped in at the Smith house to bring his mother home. When he spied this recent photo, he was suddenly attracted and said, "Oh this is a beautiful girl. I'd like to meet her." That sounded like a good idea to Auntie Smith, who had no relatives in Detroit. She was excited about the possibility that her niece might come up to Detroit and stay with her for a while.

When Mother received a letter from Auntie Smith a few days later, she was not impressed. "You tell him I'm not a traveling circus," she wrote back. "If he wants to see me, he can just come to Indianapolis."

Daddy's family was in the wholesale butter and egg business at that time. He told his family he had to go to Chicago. The trains from Detroit made regularly scheduled stops in Indianapolis, and he intended to meet Rose Budd.

"If I like this girl, I'll stay over for the weekend," he said, "and if I don't I'll just get back on the next train and be on my way." He saw her, liked what he saw, and they began to correspond that spring. In August she did come to Detroit to meet his family. They were engaged at that time and married in October of 1907.

My mother began to learn to cook, and there were plenty of eggs and butter for her experiments. If her homemade cakes didn't turn out well, she simply threw them over the back fence. She became a good cook, but she kept kosher, so there were some things I didn't enjoy until later in my life. Steak was one of these items. Jewish custom dictated that you didn't eat the hind part of the animal, so the steaks we had were tough rib steaks served well done. I hated steak prepared that way.

When I was a teenager I experienced my mother's neurotic behavior more personally than I had in earlier years. Perhaps this tendency towards difficult behavior ran in the Budd family. Her brother, my uncle Jake, was a wonderful man who was always very nice to me, but he too had a number of what they called in those days "nervous breakdowns." He would go away for a while and then come back a well man. Mother was so bright, so attractive, well liked in the community, so charming to friends, but at the same time was often so difficult at home, that it almost seemed as if she was two different people. I experienced this only after my dad died. While Daddy lived, she vented her frustration and unhappiness on him.

Daddy made light of my mother's nagging. We'd be riding along in the car, going out to collect rents or just "joy riding" as they called it then. She'd be nagging away, and he'd laugh at her, saying, "Oh well, what's the difference?" She would criticize him for not taking her seriously. He understood her; it never seemed to bother him. It bothered me terribly, however, that she was often so critical of him.

Mother was forty when I joined the family, so there was an entire generation of Daddy's sisters' children growing up while Abe and Rose waited fifteen years for a child. My first cousins, Abe's nieces and nephews, actually had children my age, and those children were the ones I sometimes played with as we grew up together. They were calling the grown ups "Aunt Rose" and "Aunt Helen," and the people they were talking to were in fact my first cousins. It made me uncomfortable that I couldn't call them Aunt Rose or Aunt Helen, too.

We were close to this family, but I did not know how close we would become soon.

In 1933, after my father died of coronary thrombosis at Shaaray Zedeck as we were spending Passover with Anna Schiller, Anna suggested that Mother and I should come to live with her family. If we wished to do that, she would buy a larger house. They purchased a large bungalow for Mother and me and all of them—the Schiller family, including two of her four sons. It was only a half a block from my school complex, a very short walk for me. And so we went to live with my aunt.

One of the boys, Abe Schiller, brought home a terrier puppy to be my companion. I didn't know much about training a dog, and that little female pup would squat down on the floor and leave a puddle. It frosted my uncle Joe Schiller. The dog seemed to like me a lot; it would wag its tail when I came in. Spotty, white with black spots, was a very affectionate dog. Mother and I lived with the Schillers for a year, 1933-34. Then my mother began having misgivings about this living arrangement. She was not happy there.

We spent the summer of 1934 at Aunt Sadie's. Mother and I lived upstairs there. I remember sitting on the stairs listening to Mother have some gentlemen callers down in the living room. One evening an older gentleman, Max Lieberman, was down in the living room and I heard him say, "I would be the happiest man in the world if I could be a father to Marilyn." He was a wealthy man with married children, very nice. He owned a furniture store and belonged to the Franklin Hills Country Club. I had friends who belonged to that country club. I think I would have been happier if she had married this man. But for one reason or another, Mother wasn't interested.

Harry Greenberg was closer to her own age. He came to visit and wanted to marry her. He was a charming man, and she liked him. He and his wife had been close to us. Unfortunately, she was killed in an automobile accident while he was driving. I think that caused some of Mother's reluctance. Harry was very good looking. She once told me she thought he was overly friendly with pretty women. I think she was concerned about bringing this man into the same home with a blossoming young daughter. Over the years she had a series of gentlemen friends who would take her out for dinner and to the movies. But all of these friendships were purely platonic. I'm sure she never wanted to be married to anyone else after Daddy died.

Just before school started in the fall, we left Aunt Sadie's and moved to an apartment on Chicago Boulevard close to the Maravilla and just one block from Shaarey Zedeck, where Daddy had died.

Religious Jews mourn for a year. My father had died in April of

1933, then Little Grandma died in August of 1934. So I was mourning two years, almost consecutively. No movies, no entertainments. My mourning was real, and I cried an awful lot. As I've said, after my daddy died, my childhood ended.

I was sometimes with my cousins' children (who were my age). Eileen Schiller and I set up a lemonade stand out on Dexter Boulevard one very hot summer day. Eileen lived half a block away from Dexter, a busy thoroughfare on which were located a movie house, dress shops, butcher shops, a fish market, and other stores. We ran out of ice on this warm day, and when we went back to Eileen's house, we found her mother didn't have any more ice.

I suggested to Eileen, "Why don't we go down to the fish market and get some of their ice?" We did. The manager was agreeable, so we just dumped that ice into the lemonade and sold all the lemonade we could make. Now I will never buy from a children's Kool-Aid or lemonade stand. If I could use fish ice in the lemonade when I was a responsible twelve-year-old, what might younger children do today?

Mother was a talented bridge player. When she came home from a bridge party or club, I was so used to her being a winner that I never said, "Did you win?" I always asked, "What did you win?" She played in a couple of afternoon bridge clubs, where these ladies would chip in their weekly quarters, keeping a tally of the winners every week. At the end of the season they purchased matching sets of prizes available to give to each weekly winner.

I still have some of Mother's awards including two dozen hand-painted fruit plates and two dozen beautifully embroidered Madeira linen luncheon napkins. Mother kept her sets of even dozens. However, she had won more than that. She gave the extras to players who had not won anything.

Mother was a talented woman. She had taught herself to become an excellent cook and loved to entertain. I admired her speed and precision when cutting very fine homemade noodles from rolls of dough she had prepared, and I loved her homemade chicken noodle soup.

And there was a beautiful dessert she sometimes made for her bridge luncheons, one half of a large canned pear over which she spread cream cheese. After cutting and seeding large grapes, she carefully placed each half grape on top. The finished products looked like a small bunch of grapes on each guest's plate with the stem left coming out of the pear below. I think she was proud of this artistic creation.

She could draw, too, and had elegant penmanship with many flourishes. For having only three grades of formal schooling she seemed to do most things better than a lot of college graduates I have known through the years! Her ability at the piano was uncanny; clearly she had an ear for music. If she was not familiar with a popular song, all she needed was for someone to hum perhaps a dozen notes. Then she could pick up the melody, improvise the bass, and play it very well on the piano. Even when she was in her early eighties and her memory was going, she could still play the piano to entertain residents while she was living at the Borinstein home for the elderly.

One thing I most admired was her ability to make conversation. She was never at a loss for words and had a marvelous sense of humor, often devising clever descriptive names for friends and relatives. When talking to others, for instance, she referred to one of her sisters-in-law as the "Big Chin." She was also good at getting friends to invite her out when she had nothing to do on a Sunday afternoon. She'd call a close friend on the phone and might make what seemed to be an offhand remark. The next thing you knew that friend thought she herself had originated the idea of coming to pick Mother up to go with her to whatever spot it was Mother had in mind.

My mother didn't need to drive at all in that day and age. If she didn't call friends to take her, she could go on the bus or streetcar. After my father died, she took a few driving lessons, but decided it wasn't for her. Fearful and overwhelmed, she gave the car to Abe Schiller. Still, she managed very well.

As Mother began to be out of the house from time to time, frequently visiting neighbors in the building or going to her bridge clubs, I had a little more freedom. I came to enjoy the free time I had when she was out. If I didn't have anything else to do, I'd read. I didn't mind being alone.

Friends came over to the house. I had many clever ideas, not all of them as good as they seemed at the time. My mother had a guest one afternoon, a distinguished woman who had just returned from Europe and had written a book. They were in the living room talking. Back in the kitchen or dining room my friends and I were working jigsaw puzzles and having refreshments, including some root beer.

My mother called out, "Marilyn, will you bring Mrs. Aronstam some root beer?" Only about two inches of root beer were left in the bottom of that bottle. I took it to the kitchen, poured the root beer into a glass, and doctored the whole thing with water and ice, then presented it to this elegant woman. She said nothing; I said nothing. I was grateful Mother never knew.

Gradually she began giving me more responsibility. Mother had been named executor for my dad's small estate. Her attorney was charging the estate for every phone call he made, and she mentioned to me a charge of $150 for balancing the monthly bank statement. I told her I had learned how to balance bank statements in one of my classes at school, so she arranged for me to take over this task. We saved $150 a month in attorney fees with my assistance. I was no longer an insignificant child.

In retrospect I see as she began to lean on me for both emotional and later financial support (when I became a working girl), I was replacing my father's role in her life in another way. As she had always vented her frustrations on him, I now became the scapegoat. I was too young to understand how miserable she must have been and I was hurt emotionally when she constantly nagged at me. I wanted to please her, but it seemed I could never do that. Interestingly, I was not aware of my inner rage; I was just terribly hurt.

When I was growing up, I did not know that it was all right to be angry. When she was reprimanding me, I was deeply hurt, and I cried. My mother in her heart of hearts surely loved me and wanted the best for me. Still, a psychologist once told me, "You must not ever let your mother live in the same house with you and your family. It should not happen. If she breaks her leg at your house, she should go to the hospital." Mother was an unhappy woman and was never capable of understanding her unhappiness came from within. I believe people can make themselves as happy as they choose to be, even if they have to "fake it." One's attitude makes a big difference in one's life.

I did have my ways of quietly rebelling. I never defied her; in those days youngsters didn't defy or talk back to parents. You didn't reason whether a specific thing was right or wrong. That wasn't done. And I was in an especially vulnerable position, with Mother as my only parent. But today, as I try to analyze how I reacted, I believe I was doing small things to protest.

My mother was a very neat person. She kept everything in perfect order and used to say that she could open a drawer in the dark and know exactly where everything was in that drawer. When I was in first grade, my father had bought me a little desk with a top, in which I kept all my valuables, and it wasn't very neat. Sometimes I would come home from school and find that Mother had cleaned out my desk. It was frustrating to find some of my favorite things had been thrown away. So why didn't I start keeping that desk in better order? I believe it was my way of defying her. I didn't make the mess on purpose, but I made no effort to keep the desk neat and orderly.

There is no question that she was difficult for me as a young teenager. By the time I was fourteen, Mother had long, emotional attacks. Sometimes she would faint and then lie in bed for a week. I had to cope with her by myself, and at these times I stayed home from school to take care of her.

That is how I learned to cook. Lying in bed, Mother would tell me what to do, and I would go into the kitchen. Then I'd go back into the bedroom, and she'd tell me how to proceed, doing the next step of preparation. Back and forth I'd go.

Because we kept kosher, I was taught to soak and salt the meat and fowl. After I cleaned a chicken or goose, I pulled away the skin and the fat, cut all of that into small pieces and rendered the fat and skin together. When this process was complete, the skin had become what we called grebenes, leaving a Mason jar full of clear yellow fat to be used as shortening. There was nothing like goose grebenes, goose skin made crispy like southern cracklings, very good, and I was glad to learn how to make such delicious food. Then we would enjoy rendered goose fat on rye! And I liked making big pots of soup: vegetable, chicken, or split pea. I still enjoy soup.

She taught me how to make an angel food cake, which I particularly enjoyed, and I got quite good at that. I would beat up the sugar with the egg whites, using a wire whisk, then add the flour and other ingredients. That was fun. I also made a very good chocolate layer cake with frosting. I could cook! There were no food processors or blenders then, no prepackaged cake mixes or Shake 'n Bake. Everything was made from scratch in those days.

The early teen years brought new experiences into my social life, as well as my religious experience. There had been no confirmation service at Shaarey Zedeck. All the boys in our Conservative congregation had a Bar Mitzvah at age thirteen. At the time of Bar Mitzvah, each boy who commits to it becomes a man in the eyes of the congregation. He has completed an intensive course in Hebrew and is eligible to read from the holy Torah. And so it was in my congregation.

For the girls there was nothing to mark their coming of age. But even then things were changing in Conservative congregations throughout the U.S. In May 1937 my friend Dorothy participated in the first consecration class in our synagogue. The next fall my Sunday school teacher told us girls we must prepare for the second consecration, which was then being organized for the following May. I was told I was to be in the second consecration class along with some of my friends. We were to elect the consecration class officers. Immediately I wanted to be president, and instinctively I knew I needed to be nominated.

I happened to be seated next to my friend June Smith. So I said to her, "If you nominate me for president, I'll nominate you for secretary." And that is how I was able to be elected president of that class. I always liked being in charge.

June lived a mile or two away, but I frequently spent long summer hours on Saturdays in her lovely home. Her father was a jovial man, quite heavy, and her mother was a gracious and beautiful woman. June had an older sister, Beatrice. I had the feeling both parents were pleased that June and I were friends.

I was comfortable with this family. June did not possess a vibrant personality, but she was a serious girl who did well in school, and we got along well together. Later in high school she majored in chemistry. None of the other girls I knew had any interest in chemistry at that time. June was reserved and a little heavier than most of my friends and not especially popular with the boys. I was surprised when I moved away from Detroit to learn that June was the first of my girl friends to marry. Her husband, Alvin Rosen, who owned and managed a Lincoln Mercury dealership in Chicago, was some years older than June.

Years afterwards, when Gene and I were in Chicago, we would make a point of seeing June and Alvin, who lived in a spacious apartment on Lake Shore Drive. When Gene and I attended the annual home builders' convention each January in the Windy City, I would call June, and she would come downtown and take me to lunch with a few of her club lady friends. As time went on she developed multiple sclerosis and was in a wheelchair. Still, when I was in Chicago, I would call. The last few times I offered to go to her apartment to visit, but Alvin discouraged me. I think before she died she preferred to have her old friends remember her as she was when she was vital.

Social activities at Shaarey Zedeck offered me opportunities I enjoyed. I was an officer in the Young People's Club and served as publicity chairman, which gave me the opportunity to write articles for the weekly bulletin. Participating with this group was a good way to meet people and make friends.

I have to give Mother credit for letting me circulate with friends. I began to go a few places with boys when I was fourteen. One was Jerry Beckman, who was two years older than I. Short of stature and having skipped a few grades, Jerry was insecure because he was so much younger than the boys in his grade.

I was also escorted to a party by Bobbie Steinberg, a cousin of Rosalie Frank's, that year I was fourteen. Then a year later I went to another party with him. This time I felt a little more comfortable being with boys.

Right after that date, Rosalie told me, "Bobbie said you have improved so much. He said on that first date you just squeaked in his ear all night." I guess I was so afraid of not being able to say anything that I just forced myself to keep talking and talking for fear he might think I was dumb.

One of the first boys to notice me had been Jimmy Roe, who was in my class at Brady School. To tell this story, I have to "flash back" to the time we were nine years old. It began when he phoned me one day shortly after we moved to the apartment on Richton and asked if I would meet him at a Saturday afternoon movie at the Dexter Theater. That theater was perhaps a half mile from my apartment, and it would take me less time to walk there than to go to school.

My mother told her friends that Jimmy had advised me to "be sure to bring my dime." That was the admission for a Saturday afternoon at the movies. The program included previews of coming attractions, two cartoons, an exciting serial, the Fox newsreel, and two double features. This was the Depression. After World War II prices began to rise sharply, and they are still escalating in 2007. Movies today cost $7 for an adult. It's hard to believe now a four-dip ice cream cone was only a nickel. Today one scoop is more than two dollars! Gas was cheap too, and to lure customers, with each fill-up the gas station gave away dishes. I still have a full set of Depression glass dishes, which are collectors' items today.

Anyway, at that time when we were nine-year-olds, Jimmy would roller skate to our apartment on Richton in the afternoons. And he invited me to the Halloween party at his apartment building on Chicago Boulevard. Daddy drove me to the party and picked me up afterwards. I will always remember Jimmy Roe. He was a good-looking boy with rosy cheeks and dark eyes, very polite. At the party they were playing a song popular at the time. The words went, "I don't know why I love you like I do, I don't know why I just do," and Jimmy kissed the back of my hand and said, "It's true."

My first romance! But I blew it. One day some time later, Jimmy came by, still on his roller skates, in the hall of the third floor, and the manager of our apartment came up and scolded him for skating on the hall carpet. I ran away not wanting the manager to know Jimmy was with me. My insecurity throughout these early years was so strong that it kept me from doing the noble thing in this case. I was so afraid of getting into trouble. I would never want my folks to think I was a bad girl! Jimmy never called me again.

Now, when I entered Durfee Intermediate School, Jimmy Roe turned up in my homeroom class. I hadn't seen him since that day I ran away. His head snapped around when he heard my name called to see what I looked like now. And I can tell you I was at a very awkward age, with horn-rimmed glasses and not much to look at.

At home I had fun and learned a lot listening to the radio. The day Amelia Earhart was reported to be missing, Mother purchased a new table model Philco radio. I spent every spare minute glued to that set and the reports that went on for days. It is amazing to me today that even after the story of her life has been published several times with much research involved and many theories advanced, it is still a mystery.

With that new radio, I got interested in Detroit Tigers baseball. I listened to every game one summer, involved with the players and imagining the plays. Once there was a double header that started at one o'clock in the afternoon, with the second game going into fifteen or sixteen innings. My mother had someone taking her out after dinner and we were riding around listening to that game, which ended about 7:30 p.m.

When the Tigers were in the World Series, Hank Greenberg would come to our synagogue for High Holiday services. One time he had to leave for a game, and half the congregation walked out when he did, irritating the rabbi I'm sure. Another time Hank did not play in a game because it was Yom Kippur.

In junior high and high school I spent more time with Rosalie Frank, with whom I had a wonderful rapport. Rosalie was in many ways a "poor little rich girl." Her mother had died in childbirth when Rosalie was four, leaving the father with one little girl, two older boys, and a new baby, Buddy, to bring up. A housekeeper, Emily, was working in the Frank home as mother of the family. Emily was largely responsible for all the children did. She surely loved the Frank children, but was like a drill sergeant, very strict.

My mother liked me to associate with friends from prominent and respected families. One day Rosalie invited me to meet her downtown for lunch and a show. Although I was already fourteen, I had never taken a bus by myself. So the day before, Mother took me on a trial run to be sure I would know how to get downtown and back home. It was another important step for me.

Later I was able to go downtown when there were major sales. Some of these very bargains I still remember. One was a silk moiré formal, bright coral, with a large royal blue velvet flower above the bust, found at a small, upscale department store. This dress was smashing, and it had been reduced to $3.00! How I loved that dress! It was my favorite formal, and I wore it for years. When I took it off at night, sparks of electricity lit up the dark. Another bargain I remember fondly I got for only $1.00. It was a simple black silk crepe dress with white pleated collar and cuffs, which were attached with snaps, so they could be removed when they needed to be washed. Whenever I had my picture taken, I chose this dress because it was so becoming.

I had known Dorothy Davidson for some time, but we had not become close friends until I was twelve years old. Dorothy attended private school, but she and I attended Junior Congregation together. We actually looked a lot alike, both fair complexioned, and each of us had a Buster Brown bob. People who didn't know us well would confuse the two of us. She lived on Chicago Boulevard too, but a mile and a half away in a large house. We liked to walk to each other's houses. Mother was so afraid I might get hurt that she never let me ride a bike or ice skate or do anything with the slightest degree of danger.

Dorothy and I liked to get together after school and share experiences and insights. Among our many activities together, we saw lots of motion pictures. Dorothy's family owned movie theaters and would take us to see a movie on a Sunday afternoon. If we didn't like the second movie of the "double feature," we'd get on a streetcar and go to another of their neighborhood movie houses. Her dad would be in the office, and afterwards he would take us home.

Her father also co-owned a wholesale grocery business with his brother-in-law. It was interesting to me that Dorothy's father and his partner had married sisters. Dorothy's mother was one of three sisters. One of the sisters was married to a prominent doctor in New York, while two of the sisters and their husbands lived in Detroit. Sadly, the first week after these two dear men retired, they were killed while driving to Franklin Hills Country Club to play golf.

I learned so much from Dorothy, who was a year older than I. Her parents had a summer home on Lake Huron, and sometimes her father would pick me up and take me out to that large, close-knit family's summer home for two or three days at a time. A dance pavilion stood near the lake, and I recall that Dorothy's aunt, Fannie Saulson, went with us to that pavilion. "Don't put your weight on a boy's shoulder when you dance," she told me. "Just rest your hand gently there." That family had so many things to share.

Dorothy became my dearest friend. We were able to confide in one another and we had the most fun analyzing our friends. That sort of confiding does not come easy, though I am able to confide in my daughters now. At that time Dorothy served as the sister I had always yearned for. I know we were as close as sisters during those last four years I was in Detroit.

When I entered Central, the high school on the same campus where I'd been going to school most of my life, I began going out more with boys. I was a short girl, and it bothered me that people thought I was younger than I was—a baby.

I recall going to a dance at Cranbrook, a private school for boys in Bloomfield Hills. The boy who invited me was short, too, but really slick looking. His father owned the haberdashery shop in the Book Cadillac Hotel. So this date of mine came in a white tuxedo, with a maroon satin cummerbund and matching bowtie, and his straight, blond hair all combed back and shiny. He resembled the bellboy in the old cigarette ad, "Call for Philip Morris." We were surely a short little couple out there whirling around the dance floor.

I really liked older boys because they were often taller, and it made me look older when I was with them. Harold Frank, Rosalie's brother, was one of these boys, and he and his date came up to us as we danced. His date said, "We've been admiring you all night. We think you are the cutest couple on the floor." I could have shot that girl. What she was really saying was, "You look like two babies." I got the message and I'm sure that was it.

I remember one special project Rosalie and I worked on together in high school. This incident shows I could be somewhat devious at times, so I'm not exactly proud of it. I really was a good girl, getting good grades, not getting into trouble. I enjoyed school and made special efforts to be on the honor roll. But I had my moments.

Rosalie and I undertook a class project together. Our history teacher announced one day that only people who turned in a twenty-five-page dissertation on a famous historical figure could possibly receive an A at the end of the semester. That sounded challenging, but I had my own take on it. After plotting together, Rosalie and I decided to speak to our teacher about our idea for the project. If we were to develop our project jointly, preparing a fifty-page dissertation, would this qualify both of us for an A grade? He accepted this idea, and we were off and running. At the time I considered myself quite clever. I had a plan.

First of all, Rosalie's penmanship was truly artistic. Mine was atrocious. I would be certain that hers was the hand that wrote the paper. Then, I wanted to be sure we had fifty pages. I found loose-leaf lined paper where the spaces between the lines were just a bit wider than standard and there were twenty-four lines per page as opposed to the standard twenty-six lines. Furthermore, I instructed Rosalie to indent each paragraph especially wide. I put my hand down to show her how much space to indent.

We chose to research the life and exploits of Alexander the Great. You may have guessed what we did next. Every time we had an opportunity to mention Alexander, we would use his entire name—in full. No place in the entire fifty pages could you find a single "him" or "his." I dictated from huge reference books. One was Heinrich Graetz's *History of the Jews,* a set of three thick volumes, which had a section on Alexander the Great. I read that out to Rosalie; we probably plagiarized throughout. Then we turned it in. I doubt if that teacher read a word of it. But Rosalie and I were rewarded with an A in history for that semester.

When I was perhaps sixteen years old, a young man in his twenties from a large and prominent family opened a dance studio. As a part of trying to promote his new business, he invited Dorothy and me and some of our friends to his opening party. I went to the opening with Dorothy and her brother Bill and our friends Jack and Mignon Hamburger. Jack drove us; he was old enough to have his license.

After the opening we decided it would be fun to go to the Book Cadillac Hotel for a Coke. When the bill arrived we were shocked at how much we were asked to pay for the six Cokes. How could we have known there would be a luxury tax for the orchestra, then a sales tax plus gratuity? Only Jack had money to bail us out. It was a rude awakening and a good lesson.

We were growing older, and some of the girls had sweet sixteen parties. Invitations arrived for me reading, "Your escort will be . . .." I always got the short guys. The Franks' housekeeper, Emily, planned a beautiful luncheon party for Rosalie's sixteenth birthday at the Book Cadillac Hotel. As we walked into the area where we were going to be served, the orchestra played "Rosalie, I love you," which had just become popular. This family also had a home on a lake in Pontiac, and once or twice a summer her father would pick me up on his way out there and I'd spend time with Rosalie at the lake.

There were things about her situation that you couldn't envy, however. Rosalie's father, who owned a large company, was a male chauvinist and demanded a great deal of his daughter. One day in the lunch room at school as we went through the cafeteria line, she chose white milk, remarking that she would have preferred chocolate milk, but it cost a penny more. She paid for her lunch out of her allowance and had to report to her father every cent she spent. The amount of money spent unwisely would be deducted from next month's stipend.

When this same Mr. Frank grew old, Rosalie cared for him most of the time. But when he died, he left everything to his boys, who then discharged her husband from their business.

The days of happy teenaged times in Detroit were going to come to an end, however. Mother and I were about to change our lives by moving to Indianapolis.

For many years my Uncle Harry Glickman, Aunt Sadie's husband who had formerly been a tailor for Selig's small department store in downtown Indianapolis, had been working at Crowley Milner's in Detroit.

Finally in 1936, the time had come for Harry to retire. After all, he was now in his sixties. Uncle Harry had a veteran's pension from the Spanish American War, so he and Sadie decided to retire back home in Indianapolis. Aunt Sadie and Uncle Harry moved and in 1937 were living at 3726 N. Meridian in a very nice front apartment unit. The next summer Aunt Sadie wanted Mother and me to visit for ten days and for that purpose Aunt Sadie was able to rent us a room near the corner of Thirty-eighth Street and Salem, which was very close to her apartment.

It was on that trip that I met Marjorie Rab, who lived with her younger brother, Jack, and her widowed mother. My mother for her part met Ida Wohlfeld, who had been a childhood friend, and they got together once more. I became acquainted with Ida's son Gerry, and we became good friends as well. He sent me beautifully written letters after I went back to Detroit, so we kept up a steady correspondence.

The following March, 1939, Mother and I came back to Indianapolis for Passover. Uncle Jake wanted us to make a longer visit with the hopes we would consider moving. I have to say that Uncle Jake was pushing us to move from Detroit. He had come up during one of Mother's periodic illnesses to help her and wanted her closer to him, in Indianapolis.

Mother never liked the preparations for Passover. She believed it was too much work to change dishes, that is to use a special set of dishes kept for use just during the Passover week. Everything had to be clean and free of leaven products, with all the cabinets free of crumbs. Those of us celebrating the holiday had to live like the Israelites, eating unleavened bread. And so, instead of hosting Passover celebrations, when we lived in Detroit our family sometimes went to a family member's house. Some years we went to Mt. Clemens for the holiday, where we stayed in a kosher hotel with mineral baths. I enjoyed the hotel, but not those smelly mineral baths!

So, in that spirit, observing Passover away from home, we headed in the spring of 1939 to Indianapolis for a month. Uncle Jake arranged ideal accommodations for that month in Indiana. We stayed with a family named Ewen, who later changed their name to Garten. This family, which had come from Germany to get away from Hitler, were strict in keeping kosher for Passover, so this suited Mother perfectly.

They had two children, a boy named Harold and a girl named Esther (later Fogle). The Gartens lived north of Thirtieth on Central Avenue. The father was a typical German, so strict with those children. *"Ein vort"* ("one word from you") he would yell if the children got the least bit out of line.

Not wanting to miss any school, I enrolled at Shortridge High School. At Shortridge I was surprised to see there were no black people in the school. I didn't realize that at the time Shortridge was built at Thirty-fourth and Meridian, Crispus Attucks was constructed close to downtown for black students, who weren't permitted to go to the white school. I was familiar with blacks in Detroit schools, in my gym and other classes.

It also impressed me that so many people at Shortridge seemed to speak with a southern accent. Their families had come up from the south to Indianapolis, many from Louisville, and these people said, "y'all." When we returned to Detroit at the end of just one month, my friends told me I had acquired a southern accent too. I guess I picked up some southern drawl.

Now in 1939, less than a year after the previous visit, Gerry, who had written to me ever since I'd been in Indianapolis the summer before, came to take me out during this month-long Passover visit. He belonged to a boys' club, the "Swanks," a group of nice Jewish boys. I met a lot of the boys, and every time I met one, I seemed to hear from him the next day or next week. Suddenly I was popular!

Mother saw I was making friends, and she was enjoying the city of her birth. We decided to move to Indianapolis. During a few days in April, Mother broke up the Detroit apartment, shipping some of the furniture and selling the rest for almost nothing. I said goodbye to Dorothy and my other Detroit friends at a small going-away party they arranged on short notice. The next day we boarded a Greyhound bus and headed on to a new home and the wonderful life that was to follow.

Rose Budd, my mother, as a young woman in Indianapolis and Abe Koffman at the time of his Bar Mitzvah in Detroit.

Rose Budd posed in August 1910 with her fiancé and members of the Koffman family. (bk l-r) Rose, A. J., Anna (Schiller); Mary Koffman, A. J.'s mother; (sitting) Fannie Sachse with her oldest son Arthur.

(l-r) Abe, Rose, Hyman Koffman (Abe's father), Fannie Sachse, Ida Schiller, Jake Budd—1910.

A. J. Koffman (legs crossed) in his early twenties in Bay City, Michigan, shortly after the turn of the 20th century.

Four ladies at Belle Isle. They are (l-r) Aunt Sadie, [unknown], my mother and cousin Sarah Lewis. The man below was a friend, Mr. Feathers, who bought my mother pieces to play on the piano when he liked the pictures on the front covers of the sheet music.

My dad with the Sachse family in Dad's open Ford. Note steering wheel on the right hand side. Next to him in front is Max Dushkin, and young Arthur Sachse is on the running board. In back (l–r) Fannie Sachse, her daughter Helen Dushkin, and Helen's son, Mike, in my mother's lap.

This B'nai B'rith banquet at the Claypool Hotel in Indianapolis about 1921 with a table of my future family seated together. Arrow points to Ruby Glick (from 7, clockwise) Fay Glick, Gene's grandfather Adolph Biccard, Jake and Kate Budd, Sadie and Harry Glickman.

Aunt Sadie with her beloved poodle "Beauty."

The Budd family gathers for Lester and Neoma Budd's wedding. Among others are (back row far l) my mother and I, and (far r) Sylvia and Clarence Budd. Front row includes (holding hands) Lester and his bride Neoma, Harold Budd, and the "mama and papa" Kate and Jake Budd.

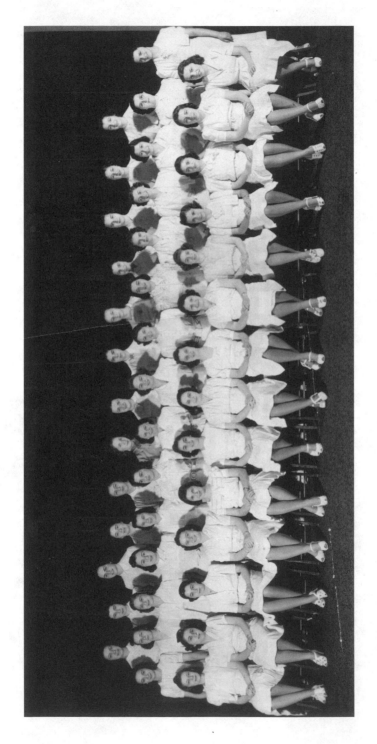

Consecration Class. June Smith (top row, third from right), Rosalie Frank, and I (bottom row, fourth and fifth from right). May, 1938.

Life is Beautiful in Indiana

3

ortunately, to provide us with new living accommodations, Mother was able to rent a nice apartment in the 3726 building on North Meridian, just a few blocks north of Shortridge, where I finished the first half of my senior year in June 1939. In Detroit I would have graduated the next January, but in Indianapolis there were no graduation celebrations or exercises at the end of the fall semester. I took six hours of postgraduate work in the spring of 1940 because I did not want to miss the experience of participating in the graduation ceremony. I loved school anyway.

How nice it was to have Marjorie Rab living in the same building. Shortly after we moved, Marjorie's mother had a luncheon for me to meet some of her daughter's friends. Marjorie and I became very close friends. Our other best friend was Annette Simon, who lived in the Llanhurst Apartments one block south of us. On October 1, 1939, we moved to 3540 North Meridian. Mother could not get along with our landlord, so we vacated the apartment at 3726 Meridian after being in it only six months. Now I lived even closer to Shortridge and directly across the street from Annette.

Some of Marjorie's friends invited me to a rush tea for a high school girls' sorority called the Deb-Ettes. I believe it was through my friendship with Marjorie that I was taken into the Deb-Ettes Club. Rush procedures for high school clubs were patterned after the selection process still popular in college sororities today. However, these high school girls did not demean their pledges. I was selected, along with Carol Rosenbloom (now Carol Bloomgarden), Gloria Strachen, who married David Baerncopf; and Dick Glasser's sister, who spent her married life as Louise Grimes in Denver. We were the sister club of the Swanks and often exchanged parties.

Later, during the war, Marjorie met a captain, Morris Fiterman, about twenty years older than she was. Since she had lost her father when she was quite young, this father figure must have appealed to her. I remember he taught her to drive, and she marveled at how patient he was. Morris was a doctor serving in the medical corps while he was stationed here. They fell in love and married, and she went off with him as Mrs. Morris Fiterman when he was transferred. He remained in the army, became a major, and continued in the service until he was eligible to receive a pension.

Morris lived into his nineties, and although they had agreed early in their marriage that they would not want to bring a child into this world, they had a long and fulfilling marriage and traveled together all over the world. They were certainly a devoted couple. And Morris seemed quite young for his years when he was here with Marjorie for our fiftieth Shortridge reunion.

Getting to know the girls and Indianapolis, was, of course, only half of my experience. I was dating a lot. I dated Gerry Wohlfeld most when I came to Indianapolis, but he was extremely shy. We went out for a couple of years, and I don't think he ever tried to kiss me, which was fine with me.

I was able to meet many boys, and many called for dates. One time that first year I had a date every single night for two weeks. The last night I went out with somebody I wouldn't normally have accepted a date with, but why not? Keep the record going. Still, the night before my seventeenth birthday, I wrote into my diary, "Sweet sixteen and never been kissed. I wonder if I ever will be?" The customs were, of course, quite different then.

I hadn't lived here very long when I had a blind date with a young man named Joe, Jr. My friend Annette was going with Bob Schwab; they had been dating for several years. Bob had an interesting and somewhat sad story. He had been in an auto accident or some other misfortune, and he had a silver plate in his head. Bob was a wonderful person, but every once in a while, he would lose consciousness. He'd pass out and not say anything for a very short while, then he'd start in again and take up the conversation where he had left off. Annette and her mother were Christian Scientists. Before I met Annette I had heard some arrangement had been worked out for Annette to be Bob's chauffeur. Soon Annette and Bob became fond of each other. So they were the other couple on this date I had with Joe, Jr.

We went to a movie and ended up at Annette's. Her parents were not at home. While Bob and Annette were in the back room schmatzling, Joe kept trying to kiss me. I had a friend in Detroit who had said, "If you kiss a boy on your first date, you are a hussy, but if you kiss a boy on a blind date, you are a double hussy." Well, we were out there in that living room for about an hour and finally I let him kiss me, my first real kiss, and it was traumatic.

The next morning I felt terrible, as if I had committed the worst crime in the world. I truly was sick. Additionally, I was afraid my reputation would be ruined, and I worried it would be all over town that I was a double hussy. I never told anybody, and he was nice enough not to tell anyone either.

For quite a while I dated another Bob, Bob Jaeger, who was several years older than I. I don't recall how I met him, but once I joined the Deb-Ettes, I was able to meet many more young people in our Jewish community. On our first date I was Bob's guest for the annual Christmas party given by a club known as the Hai-Rash (pronounced Hayrash). Bob was a member of this group of young Jewish boys, who were older than the Swanks Club boys.

The previous summer of 1939 Bob had been in an automobile accident with his good friend Sidney Netzorg, who was killed instantly. Bob took it very hard. Poor Bob was a born loser who frequently had bad experiences. Only a few months after the accident, he was mugged near Sam's Subway.

It wasn't long after the auto accident when I had my first date with Bob. We were together at the Hai-Rash formal dinner dance. Bob had been drinking a lot that evening, and I was discouraging him. I think I gave him a good scolding. After all, I didn't drink.

Later, when he was sober, Bob considered what I had said seriously. He decided to quit drinking "cold turkey." It impressed him that I was interested in his welfare, so caring. Bob didn't appeal to me romantically. For me it was all platonic. But he was much more interested in me: he wanted me to be his girl. We dated a lot, until finally I was going out with him so much that other boys stopped calling. I made it clear to him that we were not going to be a couple.

We agreed together that I would go out with him just once each month. Bob made sure each of our monthly dates was special, taking me to expensive places. He made plans he knew I would enjoy. I recall that on December 7, 1941, the date of Pearl Harbor, he took me to see the Sonja Henie Ice Show in the Coliseum at the Indiana State Fairgrounds. But it is sad that Bob had no confidence in himself. I really felt sorry for him. When Bob went into the army, we corresponded and he often sent me thoughtful little gifts. Knowing how much Judaism meant to me, one day he offered to study to be a rabbi if I would marry him, so I could continue a pious lifestyle if I married a rabbi! But it was not to be.

I liked and admired the Jaeger family. Bob's father was a doctor, and his sister, Louise, was a past president of the NCJW (National Council of Jewish Women). Several years after I married Gene, Bob married Shirley, a divorcee from Cincinnati. Unfortunately, after many years, Bob and Shirley divorced and he moved to Naples, Florida. There Bob lived in the Goodlet Arms complex owned by the Gene B. Glick Company. We stayed in touch a bit, but he is gone now.

Another beau was Irvin Berkowitz. We had several dates each week for over a year or longer, and he wanted to marry me. But he was short. Once he stopped to buy some mints, and as he was walking back to the car, I thought, "My goodness, if I marry him, our children will be midgets." Irvin was a pharmacist who eventually married an Indianapolis girl, and they had two very bright children. Years later after Irvin and his wife joined Broadmoor Country Club, he joined Gene and me one day for a round of golf.

Meanwhile, my future was taking shape.

I finished school and completed the postgraduate work at Shortridge, all college prep courses. I wanted to go beyond high school, so I applied for a scholarship to college.

I did not get the scholarship. Later in life I came across a social worker who had met with my mother about the scholarship. This woman told me that my mother did not want me to go to college and convinced her not to proceed. This was her view of it: "You'll get a man without going to college." Actually it happened for the best. We didn't have any extra money. My mother was able to pay the rent and buy her produce at the quick-sale table, but there wasn't much beyond that. And I am sure it wasn't a full scholarship that was available for me.

Mother and I were living on the proceeds of the few annuities Daddy had left us. The money did not come in a lump sum at the time of his death, and the aggregate of what this money earned was an annuity fund that paid a modest sum each month.

It was appropriate for me to work, and I did so throughout my early twenties. Mother had worked after third grade, becoming quite expert at decorating women's hats in a millinery shop downtown. I have a wedding photo in which I'm wearing a plain brown straw hat Mother embellished quite artistically with a pink silk rose.

Several times after I had joined the business world, I thought I might go back to school at Butler University. I was able to save a good deal of my salary, and tuition was low. I could have taken the bus to Butler from right outside my door.

I thought I wanted to be a social worker; it sounded good. But I am certain I would not have gone far in this work. Some years after I was married, I became very active in the National Council of Jewish Women. Then I had the opportunity to accompany a social worker on one of her cases. I was so uncomfortable with that dysfunctional family, it was evident I would never have made the grade in social work. The other avenue I considered for a college major was journalism. In my postgraduate work at Shortridge, I had taken a course in advanced composition and really loved it. I believe I would have taken more classes in this subject had I continued my formal education.

So I did not pursue college at Butler. I went instead downtown to seek schooling in a business college in the Knights of Pythias Building. They agreed to admit me if I would work in the school office to earn my tuition. After a couple of months, I realized I wasn't learning anything I didn't already know and I was doing a lot of free work for them. It occurred to me that it was time to receive some compensation for my work.

I called the Indiana state employment agency. The telephone company had an opening for a comptometer operator for which I was well prepared. I had taken a course at Shortridge that taught students to operate the comptometer machine. It took pressure to manipulate the many keys, which is why I have never had strong fingernails. To operate this primitive machine, one needed to punch selected keys vigorously using both hands at the same time. These office machines were cheap and widely used during the Depression, and were eventually replaced by electric calculators and later by computers.

I was told I should go to the telephone company and interview for a job set up by the employment agency. This was quite different from going to the business college to barter my services in exchange for sitting in a classroom. If I didn't have something to say, it would not look good, so I spoke up. This was a big mistake. It turned out that I easily passed their comptometer test and they thought they might hire me, but they were afraid I might spend too much time talking at work.

The employment agency later sent me to the Rough Notes Company, which was owned by the Wohlegemuth family. This company sent out mass mailings for insurance companies. I worked at the company for three-week stints, learning to assemble materials and stuff envelopes for their bulk mailings. We'd call it "temping" today.

It was fun at Rough Notes, which was located at Ohio and Alabama. We had an hour for lunch. I felt I had to "beat the clock" working with a punch-in-and-out time clock. The timer moved at seven-minute intervals. I managed to dash out just as the first interval began. I'd shop at my favorite department stores, grab a bite on the run and zip back at lightning speed so I could punch in at the very last second of the seven-minute system cycle. L. S. Ayres and Wm. H. Block Company were six or seven blocks away with stoplights at every corner, but I was never late. It was a challenge, great exercise, and I loved it.

Shopping downtown for what I needed, I paid for all my own clothes and my mother's, too. I took out department store charge accounts and knew how much I had to spend each month. After I took a permanent job at Indianapolis Life Insurance, the money I did not need went directly into my savings account. We were paid biweekly, and I made deposits in the bank on the northeast corner of Thirtieth and Illinois. Today you will see a huge dinosaur popping out of the Children's Museum at that location. In five years' time I had saved $2,500, a lot considering the value of money in the 1940s. My needs were small.

Before I was hired permanently, I also worked for auto loan companies, which was such fun. I got to read all the credit reports of people wanting to get loans, and there was a good deal of interesting information on these applications about people I either knew or knew about. I did that intermittently for close to a year.

My permanent job eventually was at Indianapolis Life Insurance Company. Annette's friend Bob Schwab helped me get the job I wanted most. His father was the top salesman at Indianapolis Life, and I told Bob, who was working at the company, "I'd like to work at Indianapolis Life." It was six blocks from my home, at the corner of Thirtieth and Meridian. I would be able to walk back and forth to work. "If you help me get a job there, I'll buy an insurance policy from you," I told Bob. So he did, and I did. They hired me in the fall of 1941.

The job application asked, "What salary do you expect?" I wrote down "$60 a month to start, and if I do well in three months, I would like $65." They turned out to be pretty chintzy with their employees. For each year a worker had been with the company, the Christmas bonus he or she received was a crisp one-dollar bill. Still, I enjoyed working there and I was glad I had the $1000, thirty-year endowment policy I bought from Bob Schwab.

Though the salary wasn't high, the experience at Indianapolis Life was priceless. When you have worked for five years in an office, you learn a lot about business. I got very skilled at typing, and I still love to type, and in addition I picked up a lot of information about business management.

I came to know the people there, including the executives. The president was Mr. Portius; the vice president was Walter Huehl, who was in the air corps most of the time I worked there. He later married Katherine Morgan, one of my good friends today.

I began working in the Policy Loan Department, an area of only five of us girls. People sent in their payments, and only occasionally was some of this mail outside the routine. I would attend to all the routine payments first, then take the difficult cases to the head of the department. This woman, Mrs. Martin, would dictate letters, and I would type and send these letters out to the policy loan holders.

Upstairs the head of the Reinsurance Department left, and her assistant took that job, so they asked me if I would like to become the assistant. A few years later I became head of this department. I was pleased with the promotion and the raise in salary.

Walter Huehl came back from the war and took up his job as head actuary and vice president of the company. It was customary for the head of the Reinsurance Department to be secretary to the chief actuary at the company. I had been serving as secretary to Ed Buddenbaum, who was serving as temporary head actuary during Walter's absence. As I was by this time head of the Reinsurance Department, I became Walter Huehl's secretary. I certainly enjoyed working for him.

Insurance work was interesting. Policy buyers had to have physical exams by the insurance company doctor. I saw their medical reports and read about people I knew pretty well, and although I never divulged the information, it fascinated me.

I liked the job at Indianapolis Life but sometimes felt underpaid. Just out of curiosity, I would look in the newspaper and call up companies advertising for jobs similar to mine. These jobs often offered a little more money than what I was getting.

I started out at $60, then $65, and over time there were more advances, until I was perhaps earning $135 a month five years later when I left the company. Still, I realized that though my paychecks might not have been much to brag about, I was able to save more because I didn't have to dress up for downtown. All summer I could wear bobby sox and saddle shoes to work. There was no bus fare to pay and no lunches to buy.

Mother never charged me rent and took care of my needs at home. When I walked home at noon from work, I found my lunch on the table, ate in half an hour and then walked back to work. She did my laundry, shopped for food and cooked it, and kept our apartment spic and span.

I loved walking to work. Near where the Children's Museum is now located, I passed the Rauh Memorial Library each day. I read every book in that library, delving into subjects that interested me, learning a lot about religion, psychology, and philosophy. I devoured historical novels and biographies, the classics, and contemporary writers like Irving Stone and Leon Uris. Reading in this way, I received more than the equivalent of a college education. My experience at Indianapolis Life was invaluable preparation for what was to follow.

Mother had a lot of friends, and she was still arranging to get around with these ladies for pleasurable afternoons. Still, my mother was growing more dependent on me. From the time I went to work, Mother never had to buy any clothing; I bought all her clothing then and ever after and enjoyed giving her presents. I even had a Persian paw coat made for her at the same time I ordered a brown seal coat made for myself. Our friends, the Wohlfelds, were furriers and gave us a very good price.

There were still the emotional spells. I would have to take a week off from work at times to care for Mother. And in spite of the achievements I was experiencing, she was still nagging. I wanted nothing more than to please her; pleasing her meant having her love. In retrospect, I can now see that caring for me alone, with her worry about my welfare was difficult for her. As much as it was possible for her to love anyone, she loved me. I really feel sorry for her because she was never satisfied. It is sad that she did not have the ability to enjoy and appreciate all that was positive in her life.

In spite of the emotional distress she frequently caused me while I was dating and working, I was maturing, coming to respect the high moral and religious values of both of my parents. I wanted them to be proud of me. I still felt God and my daddy in heaven were watching over me. Now, in my early twenties, I was developing inner strength. You might say I set high standards myself. In my heart, I hoped some day, if the war ended, I might find someone very special with whom to share all I held dear and important.

I took a lifesaving course at the YWCA during the war and continued building my friendships and dating. I had read Dale Carnegie's *How to Win Friends and Influence People* before and after moving to Indianapolis. "Train yourself to remember names," Dale said. I took note of that. When we came to Indianapolis, people I'd met just once, perhaps several weeks earlier, couldn't get over the fact that I remembered their names when I saw them again.

Many of the boys were gone to serve our country. During the war, from 1942-1945, I served as a USO cadette, volunteering at the Kirschbaum Jewish Community Center, located at Twenty-third and Meridian. I'd play games with the young servicemen. I remember learning to play pinochle, and I'd take them on at ping pong, playing just well enough to give them a pretty good game, but not well enough to beat them. That seemed to be a good strategy anyway when playing with the young men at the USO or elsewhere.

The lonely soldiers would tell me their troubles, and I'd listen to them sympathetically, though I hardly felt qualified. I did attempt to counsel them.

I met a boy at the USO from a fine family in Cincinnati. He wrote me a letter after leaving Indiana, telling me that it was "a horse race" between me and another girl he dated. That dilemma was his, not mine. Goodbye to him.

There was a book in that Rauh Memorial Library entitled *Girls Men Marry*. Each time I was dating someone regularly, or when it was over, I pulled out the book. I read *Girls Men Marry* five times. It stated that short men have a superiority complex covering an inferiority complex. I had already experienced that with the short boy, Jerry Beckman, whom I'd dated in Detroit. He had skipped grades and felt insecure socially. I was learning a lot about men both from reading and from experience.

My friends and I had reached the age when some were marrying. I had made up my mind that I would not marry anybody until the war was over. It really didn't make sense to get attached to someone who might be killed, maimed, or ruined mentally by the war. I can't tell you how many times I cried myself to sleep because I was never going to know what life was all about. I felt the war was going to go on forever, and I would never have a husband, never have children.

We had retained family connections with our Detroit family, of course. But we had not spent a good deal of time with them, getting together only on major Jewish holidays. When we had come to Indianapolis six years after Daddy died, we had found comfort in being with Mother's family. Mother was better off being with her sisters and Uncle Jake. It made her feel more secure. She was going through menopause when we came to Indianapolis and her breakdowns may have been a little worse because of that.

It was good to be with Aunt Sadie again. Annie Witt and her husband and son had left the south side and moved north to Ruckle Street. Uncle Jake Budd was here with his wife and three sons. Clarence and Lester Budd ran the business at 501 S. Capitol until the government bought all the property in that area for a huge new building to house headquarters for the U.S. Postal Service. Harold, the Budds' middle son, was a furniture salesman and had no interest in the family's business. Now that I was no longer a child, Lester, who was seventeen years older than I, began taking me out on dates. We had good times together, but because we were cousins, it was a platonic romance. However, there were surprising revelations to come in 1945 that could have affected our relationship.

It was when I was twenty-three, when I had been working for quite a while at Indianapolis Life, that I made the major discovery of my life.

In the summer of 1943, I had saved enough money working at Indianapolis Life to pay for train fare to take Mother with me to visit family and close friends in Detroit. We stayed at the home of Aunt Fannie Sachse, who, with my Uncle Ed, lived in the upper story of a double. Aunt Fannie's daughter Helen Dushkin and Helen's husband Max and family occupied the first floor.

Dorothy Davidson, my closest friend, had asked me if I had a birth certificate. At the time we had been reading reports of well known movie stars who were suspected of being "pinkos," because of their Communist Party, or "red" leanings. This was a short time before Senator Joseph McCarthy led hearings in Congress for U.S. citizens accused of belonging to the Communist Party. It was an uncertain time in many ways.

Dorothy said, "Everyone should have a birth certificate." Dorothy was always my mentor, so I took her advice. I had proceeded to write to agencies in Lansing and Detroit, Michigan, to obtain a copy of my birth certificate. But my birth records could not be found at any agency in the state. I was puzzled; every record in school I had filled out indicated I had been born in Detroit, Michigan. So where was my birth record?

I persisted and two years later I had advised officials in the state capitol of Michigan that I could be reached at Aunt Fannie's during the week of my annual trip to Detroit. One afternoon while I was out to lunch, the mailman came to the house with a letter for me from Lansing. Years later I learned that Mother destroyed the letter before I returned. It was important to her that I not know what it contained, an action which showed great insecurity on her part.

But in October 1945 another letter came from Lansing to our apartment in Indianapolis with an affidavit for me to fill out giving information necessary for the authorities to locate the birth certificate. I took it from the mailbox when I came home for lunch that day, excited to get this mail at long last. The clerk's office wanted to know the hospital in which I was born and who the doctor was so they could search the records properly. I asked Mother, "What hospital was I born in?" "You were born at home." "Who was the doctor?" "I don't remember." I looked at her. She had only one child.

"How could you not remember such a thing?" She just shook her head.

Next I said what was perfectly logical. "The only way you couldn't remember these things is if I had been adopted." She started to cry. It was true.

Several things hit me at once. I wasn't going to inherit my mother's emotional problems. Then there was the fact that she had told me all sorts of things about her family that I really didn't need to know. For one thing, Harry Glickman had left Sadie one time early in their marriage, and there were a few other skeletons in the family closet. Now they wouldn't be important because this wasn't really my family.

Finally, I had always believed there were no secrets she would withhold from me. Our relationship, though sometimes difficult, was very close, and it was a source of the greatest disappointment that she would not have told me the secret she held for so many years. How could she have deliberately withheld this vital information when it was evident I was persisting in the quest? Unfortunately, she was insecure, dependent on me, and feared I might leave her! I should have known the truth! Beyond surprise at this news and sadness that Mother had not trusted me enough to tell me what I should have known, I thought my adoption was rather romantic, and I was very pleased.

Now that I knew the hidden truth, my mother was able to tell me how she and Daddy happened to adopt me. They had wanted children ever since their marriage in 1907. She had two miscarriages, and either because she couldn't carry to term or was discouraged, they finally considered adoption.

I could infer the rest. Mother believed that having a child would solve all her emotional problems. It would make her happy, and my dad was always willing to please her.

God, or fate, intervened at this time. My father was an ardent supporter of the Zionist movement, and he and Mother went to a convention in New York, staying at the Commodore Hotel in the heart of the city. Mother became acquainted with the wife of the famous rabbi, Rabbi Steven S. Wise, from the Free Synagogue of New York City. This synagogue was not "free" money-wise but free in thought. He was probably the best-known rabbi in the country at that time.

"The rabbi shuts himself up in the study reading papers and writing sermons," his wife complained. "He is either out in the community or locked up in that study." She was an unhappy woman, as was my mother, who wanted a baby to solve her problems. Mrs. Wise turned her attention to good causes, and at that time it was to the aid of Jewish orphans.

In the early 1920s this fine woman devoted her time to organizing what would become later known as the Louise Wise Adoption Services Center. While commiserating with her new friend, Rose Koffman, Louise told her about this project. Then she said, "There is a six-month-old baby girl ready for adoption right now. We do not release any infants until we are sure they are developing normally. You and your husband should go out to our foster home in New Rochelle to look at this baby." That is exactly what Rose and Abe did.

Although they had often thought they might prefer to have a son, as soon as Abe laid eyes on me he fell in love. I was not even a beautiful sight in the cradle that day, as I was recovering from what must have been measles or chicken pox. My face still bore the remaining scabs. With the help of Louise Wise, arrangements were made for the Koffmans to take this tiny, abandoned babe on the train with them when they headed home to Detroit the next day. That was September 1922. It should be noted that the adoption papers I obtained many years later are dated April 1925.

After I found out about my adoption in October 1945, I felt like a storybook character. Somehow this tale seemed more like fiction than reality. My relationship with my mother was not altered, however, as she feared it might be.

Toward the end of the war, while this was going on, I continued dating a lot, with boys wanting me to go out on dates and possibly agree to marry them. In many cases they were interested in me, but I was not interested in them. On the other hand, to tell the truth, there were some fellows I found interesting and attractive, yet they had little interest in me.

In early August 1945 we were guests of the Wohlfeld family at an Elks Club picnic, when my mother and I saw the Glick family.

At the picnic Mrs. Glick invited Mother and me to their home the next evening to join a small group of friends to see photos their son Gene had brought back from Germany. He was home for a one-month furlough following the end of the war in Europe, and he was showing the pictures he had taken when his unit liberated Dachau. Gene had been so shocked by what he saw at the concentration camp, he was afraid no one would believe his descriptions of the horror of the place without the photos. The Glicks lived at Thirty-sixth and Salem, just three houses north of the door at the rear of our apartment building. Mother and I appreciated the invitation, and we learned a lot about the Glicks that night.

However, I had met Eugene before, in 1939. Aunt Sadie and Fay Glick had been friends during the years before Uncle Harry had accepted the offer to head the tailoring department at Crowley Milner in Detroit. Shortly after I moved to Indianapolis, Aunt Sadie had said, "You've got to meet Eugene Glick; he's a prince of a fellow." Gene had just been graduated from Shortridge High in June of 1939. One evening, he and his mother walked by 3726 Meridian on their way home from buying ice cream cones at Thirty-eighth and Illinois streets. I was seated on the stoop in front of the apartment. We had a brief conversation, and he moved on.

Three weeks later I said to my aunt, "I met your Eugene Glick and he never even called me." It was over six years before I saw Gene again that night at his house in August, when he was home on leave. Less than two weeks later, the atom bomb was dropped on Japan. Thankfully, Gene was spared having to go to Japan. Instead he was sent to Texas to await his discharge from the Army.

I had been staying active in our community, and my volunteering activities led me to a fortuitous evening with Gene. The story is involved but interesting. It begins with a young people's meeting at the Kirschbaum, shortly after the war ended.

At the meeting Mildred Levy, the center's staff facilitator, explained the need for a young singles club. Ever eager to be helpful with ideas and suggestions, before I knew it, I was made president of the new singles club. Whenever you raise your hand with ideas or suggestions, you find you are made an officer or head of a committee. And so it was at the Kirschbaum singles group. I found I was just as happy to take on leadership roles there as I had been in Sunday school and Junior Congregation in Detroit.

The same thing, volunteering and then discovering you were heading the effort, happened when I first came to Indianapolis to live. I had gone with friends to a Temple Teens meeting at the Indianapolis Hebrew Congregation, then located at Tenth and Delaware Streets. I enjoyed meeting new people and participating with them, and the next thing I knew I was hospitality chairman. I didn't know anything about being a hospitality chairman. The former chairman told me how to do it. I didn't just sit at a meeting and go home; I made suggestions. It took years before I understood that the leadership responsibilities that came my way were the result of all the suggestions I made so eagerly when I attended meetings. Still, I liked leadership roles and the responsibility that went with them. I think it may be inborn. It certainly has been persistent in my life, and it hasn't always been a bed of roses.

At any rate, in early November 1945, when I was at Kirschbaum Community Center for a singles meeting, my long-time friend Joe, Jr. told me he planned to visit a girl in Detroit over Thanksgiving. And I told him

I was taking my mother with me to a Sunday school teachers' convention in Toledo, Ohio. From there we were planning to go on to Detroit to spend the weekend with my Aunt Fannie Sachse. Joe offered to drive us back to Indianapolis on Sunday. I was delighted with this offer and happy to save the train fare for our return. Sure enough he came by Aunt Fannie's to pick us up on that morning. Midway in the drive we stopped for lunch at a large hotel in Ft. Wayne and arrived back by 5 p.m. As I left the car, I was so appreciative. I said, "Joe, is there anything at all I might do to reciprocate?"

He replied, "How about getting up a bridge game?" "OK," I said, "let's say next Sunday night." The date chosen was December 5. My dear friend, Annette, was no longer dating Bob. She would come and bring Mike Efroymson for our table of four. That Sunday, just as I walked in from teaching Sunday school, the telephone rang. It was Joe who said he had been out the night before with Harry Traugott, and Harry also wanted to play bridge with us.

He asked, "Do you think you could get up another table?" I agreed. I knew Harry was interested in Leah Schneider and called her; she accepted immediately. Another close friend, Mary Furscott, was available. Now all I needed was another boy. Although I hardly knew Gene Glick, I realized he had come home from service and lived close by. Since I had spent the evening at his home the previous August looking at his photos of Dachau, I felt comfortable calling his house to invite him over.

His mother answered the phone and told me he was playing golf. The weather was warm and balmy, perfect that day. These phone calls were all made within a period of five minutes, but I had no more time to pursue the fourth bridge player. I needed to have a quick bite of lunch and then take the bus down to Kirschbaum for the weekly meeting of the singles group. Surely I'd find some young man who would be able to fill in that spot.

After the meeting at 5 p.m. I was feeling desperate. I must have invited close to twenty fellows, but no luck. Before leaving the center, I called the Glicks' once more. This time Gene's mother reported he was in the shower. I told her what I wanted, and she consulted Gene through the bathroom door. "Tell her I don't play bridge," he said. She told me. "It doesn't matter," I said, "They can play any game they want."

I'm sure Gene was reluctant, but he agreed just to please his mother. I had borrowed a card table and four chairs from Mrs. Latker, our next-door neighbor. When the eight of us finished playing, I asked if anyone would like to stay and help me clean up. Gene says they all took off so quickly it was as though someone had yelled, "Fire!" But, gentleman that he has always been, he was kind enough to stay. After everything was back in place, we had the opportunity to talk for a few hours. It's amazing how much that conversation changed our lives.

I cannot tell you I fell in love that night, but when Gene left that evening, I thought, "Here is the kind of person I could marry!" I sensed he was a substantial young man capable of getting along well in his life, though I never dreamed at that time that he would be as successful as he has been. Perhaps one of the gifts I have been given is the ability to be a good judge of character. I saw Gene as kind, thoughtful, honest and caring. He reminded me of my father in a lot of ways. I was very, very lucky in the choice of a husband. It was a great blessing for me that we fell in love and have spent our lives together.

Anyway, I'm not sure if we had dated in 1939 we would have appreciated each other. I was just beginning to go out with many boys and he hadn't dated much then, either. Maybe if he had called me earlier, we wouldn't have clicked. At that time I preferred boys who were a few years older. When we finally did get together six years later, our experiences had taught us both a lot about ourselves and others and about the world.

He called me after that bridge game and invited me to go dancing the next Friday night. Gene's best college buddy, Sid Jaffe, was taking Carol Mahalowitz, and they and another couple would join us on that first date. On Thursday evening he called to ask if I would come over and teach him how to dance. Little did I know that he had been stationed in Dallas and the girl he was dating there was a dance instructor at an Arthur Murray Dance Studio. It was an excuse to get me over to his house so we could get better acquainted.

When I got there, he put some popular records on the Victrola and we began to dance. It was pretty obvious that he was a very skilled dancer. Still, it was fun, and the next night we were having a marvelous time on this triple date dancing on the roof of the Severin Hotel, now called the Omni, near where the football stadium is today.

When we began to dance, he did a trick step. I kept right up. "Most girls stumble with that step," he said, and I seemed to have passed a test— he liked girls who could follow his lead. That was it. I was in step with him at that moment, and Gene tuned right in on this girl he sensed might continue to follow his lead. This was the true beginning of our glorious romance.

After that we did a lot of fancy dancing while we were dating and later throughout our lives together. During the courtship, we would take our mothers to the Indianapolis Hebrew Congregation services on Friday night and afterwards drop them off at the Elks Club, where his father liked to play cards. Then we would go out to dance. We went dancing at the Indiana Roof, or to the Sapphire Room at the Hotel Washington. In the summer we had our romantic evenings at Westlake, the Southern Mansion, Denzells, or the Dells. What a shame it is that these fine dance pavilions are no longer available to our young people today. It was so much healthier than spending the evening in a theater watching sexy lovemaking or horror movies.

Gene began coming over to our apartment from his house each weekday morning, using the Salem Street entrance, to walk me to work at Thirtieth and Meridian. After he walked me to work, he would hitchhike downtown, because his job was at the Peoples State Bank on Market Street. We became "Bunny" and "Doc" early in our courtship. One morning while he was walking me to work, he took a cinder out of my eye. That is when I began to call him "Doc." Out of the many nicknames we called each other, as we laughed and joked together, he favored calling me "Bunny." These are the names we used most often. It was not long before we adopted these monikers, and they are still with us to this very day.

After we were married, I found a note on which he had kept a daily log of the dates he had had with me. It started with December 5, 1945, and just one month later, on January 5, he proposed.

His proposal was different. He said to me as we sat in his father's car that night talking, "How would you like to go to Europe with me?" Go to Europe? That could only mean one thing. "Yes, I'd like to go to Europe with you," I answered. "I mean it," he said. "So do I," I told him. That was how he asked me to marry him. Later I would tease him that we never did get to Europe until fifteen years after we were married.

Gene was thinking practically as well as romantically and did not want to rush into marriage just then, because he said, "I promised myself I would never get married until I had a nest egg. It will take me about a year to build it." I was not only willing to wait but eager to help him build our nest egg, and to await the time we would be married after that nest egg was built. Happy days were here.

I grew up in Detroit, but my future lay in Indianapolis. This dress I bought for $1 on sale in Detroit when I was fifteen. The collar and cuffs were detachable, and the locket was my mother's.

My outfit here was a gift from a boy who was serious about me when I returned to Indianapolis from a summer trip visiting my Detroit relatives.

*I'm at the Kirsch-
baum Center hostess-
ing for the USO with
two soldiers, names
unknown.*

*Bob Jeager and Bud Wolf were good friends who
served their country.*

Here I'm at Broadmoor with Annette Simon and her soldier friend.

We are on our way into the Kirsch-baum Center to enjoy a Sunday at the USO. The swing band leader Woody Herman has his arm around my shoulder. He was stationed in Indianapolis for a while.

*Annette Simon, one of my best
friends, was always upbeat.*

*I had Wohlfeld Furri-
ers custom-make this
brown seal coat, and
I also paid them to
make a persian paw
coat for my mother.*

While I was holding down the home front, Gene was fighting in France and Germany. Above he is shown on leave in 1944 with his parents (r) and Fay's Aunt Alice Allman.

Gene's official army photograph

Gene and I dined and danced in the Sapphire Room in the Hotel Washington.
Before too long the announcement below appeared in the paper . . .

January Bride-Elect

Bunny and Doc

4

In the winter of 1946 Gene and I went into business together. Some of this story is well known, but here is my version of our start in business. Gene was head of the GI loan department at Peoples State Bank. He had talked the reluctant bank manager into hiring him to establish a loan department to provide returning servicemen the money to buy a home under the federal government's new GI Bill. Most of the GIs were back by then, and they needed housing.

At first Gene was so eager to do this job that he offered to work without pay. But at that time Mr. Felix McWhirter, owner of the bank, was not interested in hiring Gene. However, Gene persisted and went back to the bank again with a plan. He suggested that he would like to set up a GI Loan Department. If the bank would pay him a modest $15 per month, supplementary funds would come to the bank under the GI Bill, written to provide on-the-job training for returning servicemen. Gene explained to Mr. McWhirter that the federal government would pay the bank $150 each month. This was an offer no Scotsman could refuse.

The department opened with Gene as its head, and GIs came in, each with a dream of owning a home. These GIs took out loans to pay for their dream houses.

On January 5, 1946, Gene had proposed to me, anticipating it would take about a year to build our nest egg. What better place to embark on such an endeavor than at a bank? Peoples State Bank became a land of opportunity. The very next week Charlie Havill, the real estate appraiser for the bank, offered Gene an opportunity to make a little extra money. He engaged Gene to moonlight after hours taking pictures of the homes he was asked to appraise. Each of the appraisals had to be accompanied by a picture.

In the early evenings and on weekends, we'd pile his mother, my mother and Fay Glick's Aunt Alice into the Glick family car and go out to take photos of these houses. We were paid $15 a picture, not a promising figure for the future of our enterprise. It was going to take a long time to build a nest egg at that rate.

But in March of 1946 a man came into the bank and said he was being transferred in one month and needed to sell his house before he left. It was a double on Capitol a little north of Fortieth. He asked Gene if he knew anybody who would sell the house. Gene told him, "I can sell that house for you." When the house was appraised at $8,500, he told the seller he would keep $250 as his commission and the seller would net $8,250 within ten days.

We placed a classified ad in *The Indianapolis Star*—"Brick duplex for sale on north Capitol Avenue." Then I took the calls that came in from the ad on the phone at my apartment. I made appointments for Gene, who went over there the next Saturday to show the house. Sure enough, the second or third person who walked in bought it. Gene ran the loan papers through the bank and the seller was satisfied; Gene walked away with $250. Things were looking up!

Taking pictures of homes was not going to build our bank account. Selling houses was more like it.

We opened a joint account at Bankers Trust with the names "Eugene B. Glick and Marilyn Ruth Koffman." With that $250 deposit, we had formed our first business partnership.

We began looking for more prospective home sellers. I'd call people who were advertising their houses for sale in the local newspapers, then we'd make appointments to see these houses, load the ladies into his dad's car, and go on over to talk to these homeowners.

During this first meeting, we explained our unique selling proposition and the need to have their home appraised. We knew we would have no problem finding a GI eager to buy their home, and we also knew we could sell it within ten days if they would consider offering the home for the appraised value. Once Charlie Havill had completed his appraisal, we would call and tell them the amount of the appraisal. If the homeowners were interested, we would go out to have them sign our proposition.

We gave the seller a check for $100. Accompanying the check was a guarantee that we would have their home sold and closed in ten days. Our small commission plus the speed and ease of the sale was a great advantage to the seller. Our pledge was that if we failed, they could keep our $100. That the house would be offered at the appraised value was the attraction for a would-be GI buyer.

Houses were very cheap in those days; many small homes were only $3,000 or $4,000. Under the GI bill a house could be purchased for 10% down. If the house was $4,000 and the buyer had $400, he could buy the house and obtain a loan at the bank.

These homes that GIs could buy with little cash upfront and low monthly payments were indeed what we call today "a slam dunk," a win-win situation for all concerned. The ex-soldier was able to buy a home for only a few hundred dollars down. The bank would make a profit selling the loan to the federal government and realize a fee for collecting the monthly mortgage payments for the duration of the mortgage. And the new business established by Gene and Marilyn would be paving a steady road ahead for the nest egg we were building. On a $3,000 or $4,000 house, we were glad to have made just $100; on a house selling for $8,500 or more we believed $250 was a fair and reasonable profit.

Some homeowners felt their home was worth more than the appraised value and would not sign up with us. I did not forget them. I kept a 3x5 file card box in which I placed a card for each home we had seen that was available for sale.

I would make follow-up calls to sellers who had not taken our deal when we initially talked to them, asking them if they had sold their home. Most of them had not. So I told them our offer still held, and some were now ready to sign the agreement with us.

Others told me they had signed up with Jack Carr, the leading real estate sales company at that time. I wanted to know for how long Carr had their home listed. I kept these sellers in my file and gave their cards different color tags, red for thirty-day listings, blue for sixty, and green for ninety days. At the end of the listing period, I would call once more. Then if the house was not sold, they would surely be ready for us.

Another set of 3x5 cards was for prospects who had specific preferences. Many times I had a customer who wanted a home in a certain neighborhood, or one designed just like one of the seller's homes or with a specific feature one of these homes provided. Once a seller had agreed to go with us, I would look in the box and call the buyer I thought would be most interested in their house. There were times my prospect would go right out to see the home I had just secured and decide to buy it. Then I would set up an appointment with Gene at Peoples State Bank, and a few hours later buyer and seller had signed all the papers and everyone was happy. It was all in my day's work.

Soon we were doing very well. When I look back on those days, I smile thinking of how much fun I was having on the phone contacting prospective buyers and sellers. There were times when in less than two hours I had found a seller whose listing with a company like Jack Carr had just expired. I was able to match that home-owner with a GI eager to buy that very house. In retrospect I see where we were not only making money, but also rendering a valuable public service to these young veterans.

Perhaps I had come by it naturally, because my father had been in the real estate business, after all. It was all so easy and natural for me to be working in this delightful business. At Indianapolis Life I had developed a lot of office skills that came in handy, such as the filing system I was using. I can see that my experience in those five years before I married, learning business by doing (not by being taught in school), was invaluable.

In June 1946 I recall going on the bus with Gene to the Willowbrook par-three golf course at Forty-sixth and Keystone. Gene said, "By the end of the year, we will have $10,000." That was a huge sum of money, similar to $100,000 or more today. I did not think that was possible. But that is exactly what we had made in those nine months from March through December 1946.

Prices were so reasonable right after the war, though with all the shortages that situation was certainly changing. A car was a necessity, and we were lucky. Before the war you could buy a Chevrolet for $200, but of course at the end of the war, you couldn't get a Chevrolet because there were none available. Production had been halted "for the duration." Barrett Woodsmall, who was a friend of the McWhirters, came into the bank often, and he liked to talk with Gene in the loan department. In late 1946 for a $200 fee Mr. Woodsmall arranged for us to visit the Wides Chevrolet agency to look at new model cars in the showroom. Without some social connection during this period of post-war scarcity, there was no way to order an automobile. We had to wait until the spring of 1947 for delivery of our car.

Gene was pleased and proud that I was able to become a real partner to help him develop our nest egg. As our little business prospered, Gene came to believe I would be needed full time and suggested that I quit Indianapolis Life. I was glad to do this and resigned in October, 1946.

He appreciated this, and I'm glad to say that today he gives me a lot of credit for our start in business. Originally we had planned to get married at Thanksgiving, but when that time approached Gene was wary. He said, "The government is paying for these GI loans that are keeping you and me in business, as these young people buy houses with low interest rates." Our little business was dependent on the bank's GI loans. When the bank had a million dollars worth of GI loans, Gene would go up and sell the loans to Ginny Mae (Government National Mortgage Association) in Chicago. As long as this agency continued buying these loans, our real estate business was secure. Gene told me: "The government frequently alters programs after the first of the year. Let's wait until the first week in January to marry."

And he was right. While we were still on our honeymoon, we got the message that the government had halted the GI loan program for a while.

One day Charlie Havill recommended we buy a piece of property he called a "dog," on which we could make a nice profit. After seeing this run-down shack, with an outhouse in the back, located on the south side of the city, we recognized its potential. However, we did not want to dip into our nest egg. So, after Gene promised he would never tell my mother, I agreed to withdraw $2,500 from my personal savings account to buy the place. It was no mistake. I learned a lot working with contractors to modernize this shack. What's more, we made a $1,000 profit. For a young couple about to be married, this was not a bad investment.

We did not spend months in planning our wedding, which was set for January 7, 1947. We were too busy with our real estate business—which was the most important thing to us. Besides, it would have made no sense to have a fancy wedding at that time. Our wedding was not for others; it was for us and those closest to us. We were not interested in presents. We would buy what we needed in due time.

I did think about our future life as a married couple after we came back from the honeymoon. Securing a place to live could have been difficult. But once again, Barrett Woodsmall agreed to come to the rescue. We paid him another $200 to find us an apartment. It was in Woodruff Place, but that was too far from our friends and family, who all lived in an area roughly from Thirty-fourth to Fifty-sixth street, between College and Capitol. We had no car. We couldn't live that far south and east. We would have been stranded, so we advertised, describing the location we required. A young woman answered, telling us she was living in one side of a house that was one of four small frame doubles at Forty-ninth and Rookwood, across from Butler Fieldhouse. The woman, whose mother owned the doubles, had been divorced a few months earlier. She did not want her mother to see all the cars of her gentlemen friends who were coming and going at this house. So we arranged to trade with her. She went to Woodruff Place. We came to live across from the Fieldhouse. The bus stopped right by our front door.

I wanted to cook breakfast for my husband the first day after arriving home from the honeymoon. My mother and I took the bus on a sleeting December afternoon to a wholesale supply house near downtown, where Clarence Witt knew the owner, and I bought all the supplies needed for our first kitchen at a good price. So my dreams for our first morning back were materializing.

We had neither the time nor the money for a large wedding, so we kept it simple. In those days the bride was expected to pay all expenses, and I wanted to do just that. I had saved enough from my payroll checks to cover a party of fourteen. I chose to be married at the Marott Hotel, in a small basement room with a white tile floor. The service, conducted by Rabbi Maurice Goldblatt, was planned for 10:30 in the morning.

Only a few close relatives would be invited. The Marott would serve a brunch following the ceremony in a small private room off the ballroom. This simple ceremony was what I could afford and all we needed. Gene remembers it as beautiful and meaningful. I was completely happy with every detail. Shortly before our wedding one of my Deb-Ette sisters had a huge wedding and assembled an expensive trousseau. Sadly, they were divorced within a year. A wedding is not a marriage.

I was married that morning in a wool turquoise travel suit, which I loved and wore for years. This was the first time in my life I had ever paid full price at a fine store (Saks Fifth Avenue in Chicago). Before I was married my dresses were lovely but they were purchased at sales with value in mind. I had never spent more than $10 on any dress, even if the original price may have been as much as $25. Most of the time I was able to find dresses for five dollars or less.

We had planned to take the 2 o'clock train out of town, but we lingered so long at the brunch that we missed our train and decided to remain at the Glicks' house for a few hours. Then we caught the evening train to Cincinnati, to stay at the Netherland Plaza Hotel. I had visited Cincinnati once before and was impressed with that magnificent hotel, so I wanted to stay there on my first wedded night.

Shortly after we boarded the train, Gene fell asleep. He had been working very hard during this period, so there I was, wearing my huge orchid, and the elegant going-away suit, obviously a bride. I was all keyed up, and there was the groom sleeping next to me. An older man we knew, Percy Simmons, was on the train and saw us. I was embarrassed and kept my eyes glued to a picture of Abe Lincoln hanging at the front of the train car.

After we arrived at the Netherland Plaza, we were shown to our room. I nervously crossed the threshold with the man I had just married, wondering in those more innocent days what was to come next. But Gene said, "I'm hungry. Let's have something to eat." Something to eat? I wondered how in the world he could eat at a time like this, but as I was to do so many times over the years, I told myself, "It doesn't really matter, does it?" and we went down to the coffee shop and ate.

When we woke up the next day, it was probably noon. The train for Florida didn't leave until evening (I was afraid to fly: many people felt that way in those days) so how would we spend the day? I checked out things to do in Cincinnati and suggested we could take a free tour of the Heinz factory. We toured the pickle vats and ketchup manufacturing operations. I was wearing my orchid; we were obviously newlyweds. On ending the tour, our guide presented us with a jar of olives. "Here," he said to Gene, "This will put lead in your pencil." We enjoyed the tour as well as the olives.

We were three and a half days on the train. Our compartment was comfortable, and we enjoyed wandering through the train on our way to the dining car. When we arrived in Georgia, it was such a beautiful day that we got off to take a long walk and almost didn't make it back in time for departure.

Finally we were in Florida. We stayed at the Pennsylvania Hotel on Flagler Drive, in a big, beautiful front bedroom with lovely, large windows overlooking Lake Worth. We would walk along the lake, cross the bridge and come into Palm Beach, walking right through the grounds of The Breakers to the public beach. The guards thought we were guests at that hotel.

Our routine was to get up about 11 a.m. and go to Morrison's Cafeteria for brunch. We'd have bluefish or mackerel and then go back for dinner, and every night we'd get on a bus and go to the dog track. We'd take the program and go out to look at the dogs trying to decide which would run the fastest, and then bet a few dollars. After a while we found it all quite boring. We splurged a couple of times, going into Palm Beach, once to Leon and Eddie's, a branch of that well-known New York restaurant.

I had always been told that the first week you were in Florida you had to be very careful of the sun. We tried to be scrupulous about it, not staying out too long. Of course at that time there was no sunscreen. After a week we decided to take a long walk on the beach during the noon hour. About 2 in the afternoon on the way back to the hotel, we stopped for a cone at an ice cream parlor called Pernia's on Royal Palm Way.

As I waited for my treat, my legs started to burn. By the time I got to the hotel, I needed something to help relieve the pain from a serious sunburn. Gene called the hotel bellboy and asked if he would go out and get a jar of Noxema. He brought it up, and Gene put the cream on my legs. It literally evaporated. We went through three jars of Noxema. By that time Gene had started to feel his burn. I was using the large water pitcher in the room to upchuck.

I called the house physician. He ordered salt pills and pain pills plus a prescription for dehydration. And he said, "If you are not better in the morning, I am going to have to hospitalize you." For the next several days I requested a footstool at meals because I couldn't bear to have the seat of the chair touch my thighs.

I had bought some nice clothes for the honeymoon, including a smart-looking winter white linen pantsuit. I wore that to cover my legs while we strolled again the following Sunday afternoon. As we wandered through the grounds of The Breakers, Gene said, "I'm thirsty, let's get a Coke." We went into the sun parlor, and they brought us Cokes and pretzels. When Gene tried to pay the tab, the waiter told him, "These snacks are free for the guests." "We aren't guests," Gene told him, but the waiter could only shrug. They had no way to collect cash from non-guests. There were no credit cards in those days, so the "Cokes and snacks" were on the house that day.

As we were sitting there, we met an elderly couple (probably in their sixties), and they were so happy to see young people that they invited us to a dance. The Breakers had scheduled one for the next Tuesday night. When Tuesday arrived, we got dressed up in our best clothes. One of the bellboys wanted to know where we were going, and when Gene told him, the young man couldn't believe we had been invited to The Breakers. This little Jewish boy told us, "No Jews are allowed at The Breakers." We didn't know that. We went anyway and had a marvelous time. Decades later The Breakers began to cater to Jewish clientele. They now have matzo on the table at Passover time. It is a different world.

That Tuesday was the last night of our honeymoon. We went back home on the train the next day.

After we turned the key in the lock of the house on Rookwood and Forty-ninth, Gene went directly to bed, exhausted. I began to unwrap gifts and became aware the house was getting cold, so I went down to fire the furnace, using the wrapping paper and excelsior from the gifts to start a blaze.

Houses in the 1940s were largely heated by coal. Our landlady used the cheapest coal she could buy, coming in two forms. Either it was in huge chunks which could not be ignited easily, or it was soft coal dust, which would not catch fire either. Still, I got a fire going that worked well enough for that night. The next morning, however, when Gene got up, he had to work long and hard to get a real fire going.

He came up hot and perspiring, having over-exerted himself firing up that miserable coal in the furnace. I was serving ice-cold grapefruit juice for our first breakfast and he drank quite a bit of it. That evening Gene met me at Mother's for Sabbath eve dinner. My dear husband came in looking green, suffered through dinner, and went home very sick. The heat, the over-exertion, and the cold, acidic grapefruit juice had taken their toll. How I worried that night. I thought, "It took me twenty-four years to get a husband and now I've killed him."

I called my old boyfriend Irvin Berkowitz, the pharmacist. He had to work in the drugstore until midnight, but then he brought us some over-the-counter medicine for Gene. Sleep and the medicine did the trick. The next day Gene had recovered.

We needed to get back to work. Our business had been going full blast during the year before we were married, but our real estate business was now on hold, since the government was suspending the GI loan program. Gene was still working at the bank, making less than $200 a month. Even in those days we couldn't live on that, and we were dipping into our savings to get along.

A new opportunity was about to appear. Home builders were coming into the bank, and it was evident their bank accounts were growing at a healthy pace. The construction business seemed to be a prosperous one. Gene helped one builder who had a construction loan at the bank and needed certain paperwork done almost immediately so that he could draw the cash needed the next day to meet his payroll. Gene understood his needs, and was willing and able to accommodate him.

In appreciation he invited Gene to visit his building site and see the progress on his job. Gene still tells the story of how impressed he was and how he believed he could do this, too. He especially loved the smell of fresh-turned earth. When he came home that night, he asked what I thought about going into the building business, and I was enthusiastic. Early in June we incorporated as Indianapolis Homes. We thought we'd been overcharged when our lawyer friend billed us $25 to file the papers I had typed for our new business. Gene's friend the builder gave us plans and specifications for building a small 24x30 square foot frame home. I typed up the required forms to obtain permits. Although I had no idea at that time what a two-by-four was, I copied the forms we were given. After we got the building permits, we were able to arrange financing for construction of our first two houses.

In the meantime we needed to acquire a few lots for the homes we would build. We checked ads in the newspapers. It was my job to call and make an offer. We could not afford the prices people were asking for these lots. Gene told me to "offer them a third of that price." It was embarrassing, but I did as he had instructed. The worst they could do was say no. I placed the calls and made the offers. At first they were reluctant, but I kept calling back and eventually some said, "Yes." I couldn't believe it!

So we were about to build. There was much to learn and much to do. Some building supplies were almost impossible to obtain for our houses. I was still going out for afternoons with my friends. Bridge had been replaced at our tables by mah-jongg, and I would drive to play at friends' homes most afternoons. I'd come home in the car and if I saw a builder digging a basement, then I'd stop and ask, "Could we please have your fill dirt?"

I remember badgering a man with the nickname of Sheetrock Whitey, who worked at Spickelmier's, a building supply company on Fifty-second Street at Carvel Avenue. Daily I pleaded with him to deliver some

Sheetrock, a scarce commodity after the war and in great demand. Everyone was after him for the same thing. I'd call on the phone and beg for the Sheetrock, and he'd say, "Mrs. Glick, we just don't have any." Later that day I'd drive by on my way to play mah-jongg and see truckloads of the stuff rolling out of Spickelmier's. These supplies were for builders who had been customers for years; nobody had ever heard of Gene Glick. Today I'd understand their need to favor long-time customers, but in 1947 I was furious that "Whitey" had lied to me and was not willing to sell us the Sheetrock we so desperately needed. I was insistent.

A doctor friend of ours later told us that a patient of his was having a nervous breakdown. He was being badgered by some woman who called him every day begging for Sheetrock, which his company received only in limited shipments. It was driving him crazy. I was sorry about that, but we did manage to obtain the supplies.

Gene remained at the bank for a year and a half after we started our building business. We weren't really making much money, and Gene didn't want to give up his only regular paycheck. I would drop Gene off at the bank each morning and then go about my construction management job for the day with a list we'd prepared together at the building site before driving downtown.

Our first house was in the 4600 block of Ralston Avenue, with a second one starting soon after on the northeast corner of Ralston and Forty-seventh. Our job foreman was a young man from Kentucky, and he was pretty happy-go-lucky on the job. We went out to visit the site on Saturday, and the scene there looked like the popular vaudeville comedy routine "The Builders," where some yock is standing on one end of a two-by-four and the other end comes up and smacks his buddy in the face. Not much was happening on our basement. Gene then sent me over on Tuesday to tell this foreman, "We must have this basement done by Thursday. It has to pass inspection on time." We had most of our precious nest egg invested in this project and needed to get the first draw on the construction money on Friday to meet payroll.

"It can't be did, Mrs. Glick," this young man from Kentucky said. I was so mad I drove away in a fury, leaving him there in the dust. I was two or three blocks away when I heard sirens. My heart pounded and I was terrified. In my haste had I run over him? I rushed back to the scene, and he was just fine. What a relief!

The stone mason on that job, Mr. Sedam, lived near our construction site. He had a big collie that must have been about fourteen years old and would lie around on his porch. One day that dog nipped me on the leg. When I saw Dr. Leon Levy, he said, "You watch that dog. If he dies within ten days, you'll need to have rabies shots." I went over again and Mr. Sedam's dog was lying there, completely still. Was he dead? No, just sleeping, thank God.

In November the couple buying the house at Forty-seventh and Ralston needed to move in, and we were not quite finished. We went over to Hook's Drugstore to rent a sander and did the floors ourselves. We broke even on that house, and although we made no money on it, we had gained a world of experience. Those first two houses on Ralston, built over sixty years ago, look nice to this day.

We began to build more homes, beginning construction on two houses on Evanston Avenue, just north of Forty-sixth Street. I remember one day I had a hitch and a trailer on the back of our Chevrolet. I needed to pick up some heavy cement blocks at a concrete company just north of Sixteenth Street for the basements of those homes. They loaded 250 blocks into the bed of that trailer, and I drove out on Fall Creek Boulevard, not knowing it was illegal to drive trailers like that one on Fall Creek. The Chevy suddenly popped a flat tire—there was just too much weight on it. There were no cell phones then, so I knocked on the door of a beautiful home on the north side of Fall Creek Boulevard and called Mr. Sedam, who came over quickly and changed the tire, then took the cement blocks over to the building site.

We were still living in the rental house across from the Butler Fieldhouse, but we had found our landlady hard to get along with. I had wrapped a bundle of garbage and put it in the trash can on the back stoop, and for this infraction Mrs. Hinsley gave us notice. We really were ready to leave that place where the cheap coal was so awful. I remember one night to get the fire started Gene broke up two inexpensive chairs we had by our kitchen table and threw them in the furnace to get the coal blazing.

It all worked out to our advantage, since one of the three houses we had under construction was just about ready for occupancy. So in the spring of 1948 we moved about four miles east into that 24′x 30′ frame bungalow on Dequincy Street, just north of Thirty-fourth Street. We were building several of these all-frame houses on adjacent lots. As our business grew we began embellishing our homes, adding brick, then stone to the fronts of the houses. It was as if we were building custom homes at this point. Gene and I would move into one of our upgraded homes on average every ten months and use our house as the model to show our customers.

Before buying a home most people wanted to discuss adding minor upgrades. These appointments needed to be scheduled late in the day, right around suppertime. Our tiny, eighteen-inch Formica-top dining table in the corner of the small kitchen was just wide enough for two placemats, and we didn't like eating there while the customers were close by in the living room. We began to eat out a lot, going out about six and then returning for 7 p.m. appointments.

By January of 1949 Gene had left the bank, convinced he was "born to build." We were living in a brick-front house on Riley Avenue, not far from Thirty-eighth, and one block east of Dequincy. We were building a house for a couple from Detroit, and the man's wife was coming in to Indianapolis on a Sunday to see the house. On Saturday the basement of this home filled with water: the septic tank had failed. Gene sent me down to Cohen Brothers plumbing supply company to pick up a sump pump. Then he donned the navy wet suit he'd purchased from an army surplus store and went over to pump out that basement. It was 7 p.m.; we were to go to a dinner party, and it was pitch dark as I sat waiting for him, afraid he might be electrocuted as he worked with electricity in the middle of all that water. Finally, once he had the sump pump operating, he came home knowing the basement would be dry.

The time had come when it seemed right for us to become parents. With a baby on the way, it was obvious that the house on Riley was too small. We had two bedrooms, and one was being used as an office. We needed one more bedroom for the baby. We considered one of the three-bedroom homes under construction at 3725 N. Wallace Avenue, just south of Thirty-eighth. However, I said, "These bedrooms are too small. Can space be added?" We were able to add two more feet to the back of that house to suit our needs, and then this improvement became standard on all our three-bedroom homes.

I was the interior decorator for the new family home on Wallace. I made this home attractive, but I figured we'd be out of there, as usual, in another ten months, so it didn't much matter. It was ten years and four children later when we finally moved out of that house. First the baby and housekeeper occupied the extra bedroom, with the smallest bedroom serving as our office. Later, as the other babies came, we converted the slightly larger master bedroom into a sort of dormitory with three twin beds in it. Gene and I moved into the original baby's room.

Why didn't we move sooner out to the northern neighborhood where our friends were building? You have heard of the shoemaker's wife who went barefoot. We couldn't find a suitable lot. Jim Bisesi, our engineer, who was vice president in charge of construction, would go out and inspect each lot we had selected, and he would find problems.

One lot in Arden, where there is a house today, was two blocks away from a sewer that drained onto the property. So it was rejected. I liked a lot on Sixty-second Street and was told it was fourteen feet below grade. There is a house today on that lot. We kept looking at lots; Jim rejected them. We looked at a lot on Sunset Lane overlooking White River, but the owner wouldn't sell. I began to think Gene didn't really want to build a house for us at that time.

Our first daughter Marianne was ten years old, and our fourth daughter Lynda was six months old, when we finally moved into the new home we had built. This has been a perfect house for us for over forty-seven years, and we hope to be here for many more.

When Marianne was on the way, I had to choose an obstetrician. I had wanted Dr. Howard Kahn to be my doctor, since I knew his whole family and my friends went to him. But if I went to Dr. Kahn's office near Thirty-second and Meridian, I would be seen by our friends and my mother's friends, going in and out of there. Dr. Pollock's office was at Sixteenth and Pennsylvania, across from Herron art school, not nearly so obvious. I wanted to keep my good news a secret as long as possible.

I had been a full partner in the business up to this time. Gene said, "You need to get someone to come in here and live on the place, to take care of all the housework." I hired Lulu Kinnerk, a large woman who could cook, clean, do the laundry and help with the baby.

I didn't give up cooking while we lived on Wallace. I cooked when we were between household helpers. After we moved, I enjoyed entertaining for small groups, so I took a few classes in gourmet cooking. At some point I realized that we had such a good cook working full time in our home that I didn't need to be spending my time cooking. Gradually I got away from it. Unless it's fixing breakfast I'm no longer at home in the kitchen. I'm not even comfortable doing appetizers. And we've been blessed with excellent cooks.

Marianne was born on November 25, 1949, at Coleman Hospital for Women, part of the IU Medical Center on West Michigan Street. Dr. Pollock told me to go to the hospital when the pains were five minutes apart, so we went early. When he met me there in the wee hours of the morning, the doctor told me it would be quite a while. "There's no reason for you to be uncomfortable," he said. "If the pains get bad, just ask for medication." I had a few cramps but little fear at the time. I did not think about my mother's own death at my birth. I did know I didn't want to have a C-section. I wanted a normal birth.

I heard someone down the hall screaming about an hour after Dr. Pollock left, and it shocked me, so I asked for medication. I was in labor for twenty-three hours, and I kept asking, "Is it going to be a normal birth? Is it going to be a normal birth?"

They did not do a C-section but finally the doctors did something they do not do any more, a high forceps delivery. The sides of Marianne's forehead had forceps marks visible for days after her birth. They had literally pulled her out. The next day I was overwhelmed with excitement and on the phone calling friends and family when I was interrupted. It was late in the afternoon, and the doctor had ordered a transfusion. Shortly after the blood started to flow into my arm, a nurse brought me a glass of ice cold juice. Suddenly I was cold, shivering, frightened, and very weak. It was nine days before I was able to leave the hospital.

I hired a baby nurse, Mrs. Higgenbottom, for the first two weeks at home to help me with my newborn and to teach me how to take care of her. Marianne was the first baby I had ever known, and I had to learn to be a mother. The first time I gave Marianne a bath it took me an hour, with Marianne crying and sweat pouring off me all the while. I nursed her because it was supposed to be good for the baby and that went well. Lulu slept in the room with Marianne.

Marianne was a very strong-willed child. Unlike today, when there are hundreds of books on bringing up children, there were very few guidebooks on child rearing. I had nothing except Dr. Spock to guide me when I brought Marianne home from the hospital.

All I ever wanted to do was to please this baby, just as I had wanted to please my mother and never could. Within three months I was just as much that baby's slave as I had been my mother's. I had truly never before been in a situation where I couldn't understand the fundamentals of what was needed to make the situation a success and then act appropriately, but with my babies I couldn't quite grasp what I should be doing. By the time I was struggling with three toddlers, I finally went to a psychiatrist who helped me cope and understand how to handle Marianne and the other two girls. He pointed out how my own childhood was influencing my approach to these children. The anger I had held deep inside, repressed during those disturbing years with my mother, suddenly erupted.

I had thought, "Someday I'll be a mother, and then I'll be the boss," but that didn't happen. I was so frustrated as a new mother that I trembled in rage and frustration, experiencing anger at a conscious level for the first time in my life.

Children are so different, showing their personalities at a very early age. Our granddaughter Jackie's youngest, Jessica, is so docile, a moving-picture version of what I thought babies should be. Jackie is the oldest of five children and studied to be a teacher at Indiana University. So she was well prepared, but she has difficulty at times with one strong-willed child, too. Her Allison reminds me of Marianne as a small child, gorgeous, smart as a whip, and very dominant. From the time she was two and a half, I could tell Allison was born to be a leader.

Early in March 1950, less than four months after Marianne was born, we had an open house, using our home on Wallace as in the past. Each time this baby was hungry, crying to be nursed, I excused myself and nursed her behind the closed bedroom door while the open house went on.

I was still involved in our business, though it was more challenging to do both jobs. I had been doing all the bookkeeping, and a month after our daughter was born, I didn't have the checkbook balanced. Gene decided to hire someone else to come in and take over that job. Gradually over the months and years my business responsibilities diminished and were taken over by others, so I've always jokingly remarked that once he could afford professional help, he didn't need me any more.

My mother nagged that we should move the office out of the house. Soon we agreed, and Gene moved his office out to one of the projects he had going in the neighborhood.

I didn't play cards or mah-jongg any more, but I was active in woman's groups. The first year I was married I solicited for the women's residential division of United Way, then the Community Chest. I was assigned a low-income neighborhood on Thirtieth between Michigan Road and Capitol Avenue, where I knocked on doors and asked for contributions.

The next year the cards were for homes in Williams Creek. When I went to a captain's meeting and read the canvassing cards they passed out, I saw they advised, "Ask for $10." It seemed inane to me to go into that affluent neighborhood and ask for only $10.

In the 1950s I was interested in Hadassah and the Temple Sisterhood but did only occasional chairmanships for them. I began to be active in the National Council of Jewish Women, and when I was publicity chairman I took my portable typewriter with me to all sessions of a regional meeting, so that I could feed releases to the newspapers and television stations throughout the two or three-day seminar. I loved organizing all the publicity and working closely with the media.

When I first became a publicity chairman, the newspapers offered a seminar for the publicity volunteers, a breakfast at L. S. Ayres. The society editors of *The Indianapolis Star, News,* and *Times* told us exactly how to contact the paper and how to write a release, and I thoroughly enjoyed it. I called on Gilbert Forbes, the local TV newscaster, arranging for him do stories on NCJW. He even put the Borinstein Home Chanukah party on a 10 o'clock newscast for me.

As for our religious life, when I married Gene I felt it was best for us to worship with his family at the Reform temple, Indianapolis Hebrew Congregation. Gene didn't know a word of Hebrew; otherwise we would have attended Beth-El, where I had taught Sunday school for six years before I was engaged to be married. Some of my friends in Detroit had joined both Conservative and Reform groups. Reform Jews observe only the first day of all holidays, while Orthodox and some Conservative Jews observe two days on the more holy days.

When Indianapolis Hebrew Congregation moved north from Tenth and Delaware to Sixtieth and Meridian, laying the cornerstone in 1956, they sold the old building to Reverend Jim Jones, who some years later took his congregation to South America and induced them to commit suicide.

I had always kept kosher before my marriage and continued to do so for about six years. As part of the dietary restrictions, it was necessary to keep two sets of dishes. One set was for fish and dairy meals while the other was used for meals where meat or fowl was served.

Early in our marriage, it was easy to follow the rules. I had two starter sets of porcelain dishes. However, once I had help in the kitchen cooking the meals, it was much more difficult. When I found the cook had made a mistake, such as serving meat in a dairy dish, it was no longer kosher, so I would throw the dish in the trash can just outside our back door. While Gene still maintained an office at our house, he sometimes opened the trash can to dispose of waste. Seeing a few dishes there, he'd ask me, "What's this?" I would answer, "It's *traif.*" This means unclean—not kosher.

Another factor in my decision not to keep kosher was that when I was pregnant with Arlene, we went to Florida for the month of February. The following February on our month-long vacation in Florida, I was pregnant again. There was no kosher meat available in Palm Beach restaurants. At that time, for the sake of the baby, I ate non-kosher meat. When I returned to Indianapolis after having "sinned," eating non-kosher meat, I felt like a hypocrite. I was no longer strictly kosher. Some friends kept their homes kosher, but ate differently when they went out. I was a purist. I couldn't do it that way.

My mother was in the picture constantly when we were a young family. I promised myself that my husband would always come first in my life. I thought Mother made a mistake not to go with my father to Montreal when he won that trip with Travelers Insurance Company, and I always hated the way she nagged my dad. Still, it is natural to pick up habits from one's parents. The very first time Gene came home late, I was angry and began to scold. It was then he told me he didn't want to be married to a "fishwife." He was right, and I happily agreed not to be a fishwife. I'm so glad he nipped this behavior in the bud. I would have been miserable if we'd fussed and argued. I would say because of this agreement, we have had the happiest marriage possible for all these sixty-plus years.

When I got married, Mother was able to find a reliable lady, Minnie Cohn, to live with her, so she was not alone. They would go every afternoon to the grocery store, often buying groceries at Mother's favorite half-price table. Mother had a routine. She did her housework in the morning. Then, after lunch, she napped for a while. Refreshed, she'd go to the grocery store at Thirty-eighth and Illinois Street to Taylor's market or the A&P. When Minnie left, Mother obtained another helper, Odie, to live with her.

My mother was part of our family group, which included Gene's parents. If Fay and Ruby were going somewhere with us, they included Mother. Every Friday I'd pick my mother up after I left the beauty shop and take her shopping for things too heavy for her to carry. From there she always came to our house for Friday afternoon and our traditional family Sabbath dinner.

My mother was very proud and independent and didn't want to be a freeloader. She'd make dishes she liked to cook and bring them to dinner, including her wonderful soups and our favorite cherry pie.

When I became pregnant the second time, I chose Dr. Kahn for my obstetrician. Dr. Kahn said I should not go to the hospital until I really was ready to deliver. He wanted me to stop off at his office on the way to the hospital to be sure the time was right. I had contractions all day and then went to the hospital. Arlene came quite quickly, shortly after I arrived at Coleman Hospital.

With the arrival of Arlene, we furnished the former office as a nursery. When Alice was born thirteen and a half months after Arlene, she was placed in our little nursery, and Arlene's crib was moved into Marianne's room. We had to put the dining table into our living room so our live-in help could sleep in the dining space. It always amazed me that when I brought a new baby home, the older toddler always looked so large compared to the tiny new infant.

It's clear now to me that Arlene was cheated out of being the baby of the family. Arlene was born on July 1, 1952, and Alice came just a year and one month later on August 18, 1953. At about the same time each evening, two "babies" would cry to be fed and both were bottle-fed. Arlene weighed over thirty pounds, and Alice was easier to handle. I'd take the little baby and have the housekeeper give Arlene her bottle. I can see now that was very frustrating for Arlene. She began to bite others because she was angry.

I remember being on the kitchen phone one day and seeing Arlene come in and take out a can of Campbell's soup from the bottom of a cabinet. I had taken Alice, a three-month-old, out of the baby's room for the first time and placed her in a buggy in the living room. I said to the person I was soliciting for some charity, "I'd better go see what Arlene is doing." There she was, standing up on the wheels of the carriage, with that soup can ready to go into the buggy, poised to strike like Abraham over Isaac. They got along well later, but Arlene was extremely frustrated in those early days. Later the girls told me that Marianne would lock Arlene in the bathroom when her friend Judy Braun came over because Arlene would bite Judy. Judy was afraid of Arlene.

It was difficult to give each child the individual attention she deserved. But I tried. When Arlene was in nursery school, I'd take Alice out alone, and we'd go over to Eastgate and have cherry pie, which she loved. Then when she was in nursery school, I'd take Arlene out for some one-on-one time.

Alice turned out to have a disposition much like her father's. She was more easy-going and never did anything that wasn't comfortable for herself. When we would go into the shoe store and try on shoes, Alice wouldn't accept the shoes that were put on her feet. She cried until the clerk found larger, more comfortable shoes.

When Marianne was ten, I thought it would be good for her to learn to ride at the Armstrong Riding Academy over on Arlington Avenue near Forty-second Street, a short distance from our home. I took her and the other girls out to ride, and Marianne did not want to go back the next week. But Arlene did. She was a daredevil anyway, thrilled to be up high on those horses. Every week she took a lesson until she reached a point where she was cantering as I watched her bouncing off the seat, not gripping the horse with her knees or legs.

"How does she stay on that horse, Mrs. Armstrong?" I asked. "Sheer balance," she said. "She's not strong enough and her legs aren't long enough to grip the horse with her heels." I was in the early stages of pregnancy with Lynda, and I thought, "What if Arlene should fall off? If that should happen, it would scare me so badly that I might lose the baby." So that was the end of her horseback-riding lessons. Years later, when she was married, Arlene bought herself a horse named Cadillac (because of its smooth ride). They had that horse for years. Although Arlene was a derring-do, her mom was a fraidy cat.

It seemed to me that Gene should have a son to move into the business some day. I decided we should have another baby to take over the Glick Company at that time in the distant future when Gene retired.

Lynda was born on September 12, 1959, a sweet-natured, easy baby. From the very first day, we were all so happy with her that I never once regretted having this adorable little girl. In thinking of it now, I believe it would have been a great challenge for me to raise an athletic and rambunctious boy after ten years of learning to care for my daughters. It all turned out for the best.

The decade had seen me pull back from active involvement in the business, now the Gene B. Glick Company. By 1961, with increased promotional expertise at work and building National Homes, the company in one year built 1,111 dwellings. I was still involved to some extent, helping Gene select the lots they were considering and talking over the business matters with him as we always had. Although I was there for special project openings, I was no longer the interior decorator. Virginia Landman now picked out the furniture with the decorator Jack Pomeroy at L. S. Ayres. One Saturday morning, just hours before a grand opening, I was on the site with Gene and felt some patio furniture was needed. I rushed downtown, made a selection from what was immediately available, and had it delivered before noon that day. Through all these years I have always maintained an interest and pride in the business that Gene and I built, but these were the years when I was bringing up our four beautiful daughters, and that was demanding enough.

The wedding ceremony January 7, 1947.

Traditional kiss.

Mr. and Mrs. Eugene Glick.

It's official. Lester Allman (Aunt Alice's son) and Ruben Glick look on while Rabbi Maurice Gold-blatt signs the ketubah mar-riage contract.

We lingered over brunch at the Marott Hotel. My hat was embellished by my mother, who had worked as a milliner's assistant when she was a girl.

After the celebration, (l–r) my mother, Aunt Alice, in front of Aunt Louise (Morris Glick's wife), and the two of us. We missed the 2 o'clock train to Cincinnati, so we spent the afternoon with the family on Salem Street until time to catch the next one.

Our first house under construction in 1947 looked like this.

Ruby and Fay celebrated their thirtieth wedding anniversary in October 1947, not long after we were married.

I remained involved in the business for quite a while. Here I am at an open house for a new home on East Twenty-first Street. 1957.

Marianne and Allen lived on Moeller Road in one of our successful subdivisions. They occupied the first unit on the right when they came home in August 1969.

Newborn Marianne was bright-eyed at three weeks.

Marianne and I are on the beach in Florida in 1951.

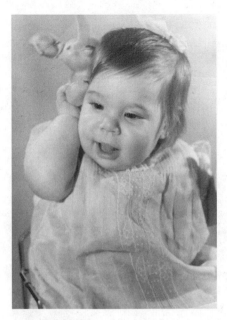

Arlene in 1953.

After Alice was born, we took a Caribbean cruise without children. We were much younger than any of the other passengers. I won a prize on costume night dressed as a French maid. Gene, costumed as Martha Washington, was bored.

These leopard swimsuits were part of our little girls' childhoods. With me are (l–r) Alice, Arlene and Marianne at the Atlantic Ocean.

Arlene, Alice, and Marianne at home on Wallace.

The year Marianne was ten, I was chairman of the Mother's Day luncheon at our temple. We were asked to pose for this photo.

When we thought our family was complete, we went to a professional photographer. Years later we added Lynda's picture (upper left) to this scene. Note Gene's fingers in my hair. He was always one for pranks.

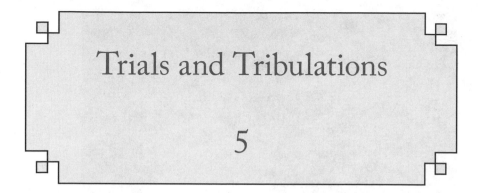

Trials and Tribulations

5

When our baby Lynda was born in 1959, we still lived in the same 1,265-square-foot house we had enlarged to accommodate our first baby in 1949. Now our three oldest daughters were sleeping in twin beds lined up side by side in one small bedroom, while the baby occupied the original office. We had been looking for lots and finally found one that suited us and met Jim Bisesi's high standards. I worked with Marion Cordill, our architect, to design a home with an upstairs, downstairs, and a beautiful spiral staircase.

I thought it would be the home of our dreams. Every day Marianne used to watch a television show featuring a beautiful and elegantly dressed bride. Each about-to-be-married, radiant young woman would make a dramatic entrance gliding down a huge winding staircase to receive fabulous gifts. I could just imagine Marianne some years in the future coming down the staircase at her own wedding in this house.

One day, however, Gene looked at the plans. "We're not going to like that up-and-down-stairs. We really should have a one-story ranch house." Then he met with the architect, and in no time they drew up the plans for what was to be the ideal space for our busy family, all beautifully landscaped with trees and flowers.

Our home was all but complete when Gene's mother died. Fay suffered from high blood pressure and had a massive stroke. At six o'clock one morning our phone sounded an alarm and we were informed that she had been taken to the hospital. Gene and I dressed quickly and drove down to Methodist Hospital at Sixteenth and Capitol. We rushed into the room where she was lying, hooked up to all kinds of machines. Gene's dad Ruby, a diabetic, needed to eat and walked out to get some breakfast.

Gene told me he had better go get a haircut. I was left alone there with Fay. I watched all the natural color drain from her face. She died, as I sat there alone with her. What an eerie and sobering experience.

We had to face the task of moving into our new house near Williams Creek less than a month after Fay died. Gene took her death stoically. He had been traumatically affected at age six, when his grandfather Adolph Biccard died. And when Gene was ten, he lost his grandmother, Rachel Faust Glick. Then his brother Arthur died in his early teens of spinal meningitis. Arthur was just a year and a half younger than Gene, and they had been very close. Gene learned to keep pain and strong emotions to himself. It is amazing to me that he even allowed himself to express the love he felt for me so sincerely and so very deeply.

I was keenly aware of this in the spring of 1963, when I had a thyroid operation to remove a nodule that the doctors thought was malignant. For six days we waited anxiously for the pathologist to examine every single cell as I tried to prepare myself for handling the worst news. It was with grateful relief we heard all was benign. This report was unexpected good news. When I came home I could tell Gene had been under tremendous emotional strain. In the past he had lost many of those he had loved most, so I could understand how much he had suffered. That night I sensed his relief—a release of the tension and anxiety he had suffered while I was in the hospital. A dark cloud had vanished, and our future looked bright. In joyous love we continued our life together with our four beautiful daughters. Once more we had been blessed.

During the first week of February 1960, we moved into our north side home in the Spring Mill neighborhood. Life improved in so many ways in this new house. The neighborhood was ideal for our girls. The Rabers were directly across the street. Their daughter Marcia Raber was a year older than Marianne and her sister, Sally, was two weeks older than Arlene. Fred and Dolly Falender had been good friends of ours for years, and they were now next door. Their son Steven was Marianne's age, and daughter Elaine was three weeks younger than Arlene. Fred was in the building business as was Stanley Herman, also a friend before the move. Stanley and his wife June were living in the third house north across the street. Their Nancy was a year younger than Alice, and her brother Tom a year older than Lynda. Our children were never at a loss for playmates.

The girls loved their baby sister Lynda and took charge of her when they were not in school. Gene built an ice skating rink on the back patio, and they taught Lynda to ice skate when she was three. Alice and Arlene were close friends but full of rivalry. Alice would often come to me complaining about Arlene. We would sit on the sofa for heart-to-heart talks, and I'd encourage her to tell me what bothered her. "I don't want Arlene to live here. Why does Arlene have to live with us?" she wanted to know.

One day Arlene came home from her Girl Scout meeting eager for me to sign an application for her to spend ten days at Girl Scout camp. Pleased, I told her she had my approval. The next thing I knew Alice came to me, whining. "I don't want Arlene to go to camp," she said.

During this heart-to-heart session I reasoned, "Alice, I thought you'd be so happy to have Arlene go away. She'll be gone for two weeks."

"I know," she said. "I didn't want her to be here. But I don't want her to be having a good time."

After Lynda learned to walk, then grew into an adorable little girl, I hardly ever had to censure her, because she was always so good and did what was expected of her. There was nothing mischievous about her. She was very sensitive and beautiful, though for some reason, she never recognized how very beautiful she was and she still is!

The first three girls had gone to kindergarten at Thirty-fourth Street and Emerson Avenue. I remember watching Alice walk into that school, realizing she moved her legs just like her dad. After we moved, the girls all attended Spring Mill School.

The only one who presented any difficulty was Marianne. Her strong, dominant personality continued to challenge me. I had to learn a lot along the way as she grew into young womanhood.

My mother and Odie, her companion, continued to live in the apartment at 3540 N. Meridian Street and to be involved in our lives, particularly the Sabbath dinners.

Through the 1960s I continued to participate in various secular women's charitable groups, as well as a number of Jewish women's organizations. The United Jewish Appeal became a focus of interest for me during this period. Sara Goodman was actively involved in UJA, as well as many other community organizations in Indianapolis. This club woman was responsible for bringing Ferdinand Schaeffer to this city to conduct the very first Indianapolis Symphony Orchestra.

My Detroit cousin Carl Schiller's wife Rose was also active in United Jewish Appeal, and Lil Diamond was a past president of the Detroit chapter of Hadassah. Sara Goodman had met Rose Schiller at UJA meetings in the U.S. and in Israel. She also knew Lil through their mutual interest in Hadassah. Rose, Lil, and my cousin Helen Dushkin made a trip to Indianapolis to see Mother and me in the early 60s. I was proud to show off my new home. Thirty years earlier I'm sure these ladies had felt sorry for me when my dad died (poor shy little Marilyn). I was especially pleased that Lil could come to see how well I was living with four adorable little girls, a successful husband, and a big, beautiful home.

When I was a young teenager living in Detroit, Mother and I would accompany Rose once each summer when she drove up to spend the day in Kingsville, Canada. We were Lil's guests at her magnificent summer home facing a large lake and situated on acres of land. As we drove up the drive, approaching this elegant estate, I was impressed with this castle on the water. I thought this place was the ultimate. Now, thirty years after, these cousins, the ones Sonia, Eileen, and Marcia had called Aunt Helen, Aunt Rose, and Aunt Lil, were here at my lovely home. It was as though we were now contemporaries. To entertain them, I invited Sara Goodman to have lunch with Mother and me, and to reciprocate, Sara entertained us in her home on West Kessler Boulevard.

Not long after my cousins returned to Detroit, Sara Goodman arranged for me to become involved with raising funds for local community services and the United Jewish Appeal. I organized a group I called the Pacesetters. I was asking my friends to increase their annual Jewish Welfare Federation gifts in the women's division of $10 or $15 to $350. Each year UJA hires on retainer a well-known author to travel throughout the country. While I headed the Pacesetters, these celebrities were an added attraction for the ladies invited to my parties, where they were encouraged to raise their level of giving. Today throughout the U.S. women making large annual contributions to their local JWF are known as Lions of Judah.

We've also invited friends and patrons to cocktail parties on occasional evenings after symphony concerts, which was always a pleasure.

Another call to serve the community during this time had come from Fred Falender's mother, Bertha, and a few of her friends interested in the Borinstein Home just north of Thirty-fourth Street on Central Avenue. In the early 1960s a small group of Bertha's friends had been raising money among themselves to buy items needed at this home for the older residents. Bertha invited me to her home, where these dedicated ladies had come to explain the need for younger women of my generation to become interested and involved. Plans were being completed for construction of a much larger facility to replace the Borinstein Home, a facility to be known as Hooverwood. The new complex would be located at 7001 Hoover Road. Because I had a wide circle of friends and my mother had recently moved into the Borinstein Home, they felt I was their prime candidate. Once the new building was up and running their vision of it was more than fulfilled. Hooverwood has earned and maintained an A-1 rating while serving our entire community, Jews and non-Jews alike.

I agreed to accept the challenge proposed and enthusiastically went about formally organizing the Borinstein Home Guild. I was installed in 1966 for a two-year term as president.

The success I've had with fund-raising as an adult may have been inspired by the successful experience I had as a seven-year-old on JNF Flower Day. From that time forward I was aware of my father and his family's leadership roles in charitable organizations. Even Clarence Budd's wife, Sylvia, had been a president of Hadassah in Indianapolis. So it was only natural for me to do the same.

During the two years I was president of the Borinstein Home Guild, 1966 and 1967, I built the guild membership up to 1,200. I wrote newsletters and set up many recreational activities for the residents, entertaining programs such as birthday parties and field trips. For one afternoon each week I recruited volunteer teams driving their own cars to take residents on outings, to places like the zoo, which was then at Washington Park; to Glendale shopping center; or even to a turkey farm just before Thanksgiving. Today insurance liability would prohibit volunteers from serving in this way.

On the home front, as the older girls were entering their teens, Marianne's strong will and dominant personality continued to cause difficulties. By the time she was in junior high, we decided to send her away to a good school in Pennsylvania. Sylvester Stallone was one of the students at the school and she knew him well.

Marianne became very fond of a boy she met at that school. He was a good, bright, talented, athletically inclined Jewish boy. We liked Allen, but Marianne wanted to marry him. Of course we had reservations. They were so young. We subsequently learned he had a bipolar disorder. She enrolled at Stephens College, still in love with Allen.

On Sunday, August 28, 1968, our life turned upside down.

It was just before school started. All the girls had come home from Camp O-Tahn-Agan in Three Lakes, Wisconsin, where our older girls had been counselors. Marianne was now eighteen and was preparing for her sophomore year at Stephens, staying close by phone to Allen. The day before Lynda had gone downtown with me to buy outfits for the fall semester.

I had a new cook, one who came with a very good recommendation from Mrs. Warren Atkinson, whom we knew. I was especially pleased because this cook was willing to work on Sunday. She had been with us only ten days. On that Sunday morning I took her to church and then picked her up when the service was over. While she was in church, I shopped for the groceries we needed for our Sunday evening meal. After we unloaded the groceries, Gene and I went to Broadmoor to play a round of golf. Lynda was already at the club playing in a kids' tennis match, while Alice and Arlene were sleeping late.

We were on the third hole of the golf course when the pro, Noel Epperson, came out to tell us we had better go home. Our house was on fire. We left the club immediately. As we approached our subdivision, we saw an ambulance at the foot of the drive. I could only think Arlene and Alice must be in the ambulance. But as we drove up the hill, Marianne, the two girls, and our dog Mr. Calabash appeared, coming down the road. The ambulance had been waiting in case some fireman might be injured.

At that moment the worst of the frightening dream was over, and I was overwhelmed with joy. Thank God our children were safe! Let the house burn, it really didn't matter. Neighbors came over to be with us as we all drank lemonade. I was so grateful. Our family was intact.

How had it started? The cook had started the fire by setting a match to our paper chute. She had mistaken it for an incinerator.

Let me explain this sorry tale. Adjacent to our kitchen was a small closet concealing a waste paper chute. In the basement below this paper chute, we kept a large basket to hold whatever fell through the chute. Next to this basket was a big, heavy cast-iron incinerator. Every Monday our part-time houseman emptied the basket into the incinerator. He then lit a fire which had its exhaust through the flue extending from the basement up through the closet and out over our roof, providing a perfect draft.

The chute was stuffed to the top with paper. The irony of the story is that whenever I shopped downtown, I never carried packages home because in those days the department stores delivered packages right up to the door. However, in this case Lynda wanted to show her sisters all of the pretty things we'd bought, so we toted everything home in big paper shopping bags. All those bags and tissue had gone into the chute.

On the preceding Friday, I had taken the new cook to the basement to show her how the waste paper/incinerator system was set up. And I specifically explained to her that our houseman, Ed Jenkins, came in each Monday to burn whatever trash had accumulated from the paper chute. What a shame she had dismissed the training session I gave her that day. Perhaps she had once worked in an apartment where the trash chute burned constantly, as I had seen in the apartments where I lived years before. When the cook saw the chute was filled to the brim, she fetched a match to get a fire going. With this perfect draft, the blaze began instantly.

It was Alice who discovered the fire when she was about to place some waste paper in the chute. With the fire raging, she summoned Marianne and Arlene. The cook did not want to leave the house. She simply did not understand what was happening. Later in the afternoon, the Falenders' housekeeper offered to take her home, but she refused, saying, "Oh, I can't leave. The Glicks are having a dinner party here on Thursday."

After seven hours the fire was out. Then we began to face the many problems begging for decision and action. The immediate question was where we would live. Gene and I slept in a motel. The next day our handsome white standard poodle went to a kennel, and Gene and I went to his dad's to sleep. For the next three nights Marianne and the two older girls slept at the Falenders' next door. Lynda was closer to the Larman children, Karen and Philip, so she slept there, just across the cul-de-sac.

The physical damage made the house unlivable—totally impossible. In Lynda's bedroom the floor had collapsed and her bed fell down into the basement. Part of the roof had fallen into the living room. Some things survived, including a certain beam that we had wondered about all the time we were in the house. Marion Cordill, the architect, had originally ordered two enormous support beams for the living room. They had come from Puget Sound in the state of Washington, the only place where this size lumber was available. The beams had been placed across the living room ceiling, and we often laughed, saying we hoped one of those beams didn't fall down on the guests seated on the sectional below. These big beams made it through the fire unscathed.

The worst thing was getting the smell of smoke out of the house. Some family photos were ruined; others were saved and others were restored later at L. S. Ayres. There was a large picture of some ancestor of the Glicks. Neither Gene nor his dad knew who the handsome old man was, so regrettably, we threw him away. Most of all Gene would come to miss a ceremonial sword that had belonged to his grandfather, Adolph Biccard. It was not ruined in the fire, but it had gone to Mr. Samuels's decorating studio warehouse to be restored, and someone must have picked it up down there.

Some things seemed fortuitous. I'd had a disappointment about a certain painting I'd wanted to give Gene for his birthday on August 29. Mr. Kamizar, owner of the King Cole restaurant in the Guarantee Building downtown, had a painting on his wall that Gene had loved. We often dined at the King Cole. Every time we were there we would admire this painting of a classic English scene, with a garden and a little girl and her dog. I had the painting appraised, but Mr. Kamizar did not want to sell it. "I would just have to replace it with a similar painting, and I don't want to do that," he said, so I could not buy the picture. It was just as well, because it would have been ruined. My meeting with Mr. Kamizar was just three days before the fire.

The winter before this Arlene had caught a sailfish in Florida and we had had it stuffed. I had believed Arlene might have this sailfish the rest of her life. It was destroyed in the fire, too.

I had stored all my prized winter wear in plastic bags, but the cleaning company drivers came to the house and removed all the plastic and stacked wet clothing over dry clothing in a pile on the floor. Most of the wool garments shrank and all the colors faded from one garment to the other. Everything was cleaned, but nothing was fit to wear. Marianne had all of her clothing packed and ready for return to Stephens, but none of it could be salvaged either. We all did a lot of shopping right after the fire.

As I worked at the house just after the fire, trying to take things out of the drawers in my dressing room, Marianne walked in with Allen Davis behind her. She had been so upset Sunday when the house was afire that she called Allen, who was home in Boston, and asked him to come right out—she needed him here. With all we were handling, Allen was hardly what Gene and I needed.

With all of this intensive work, I lost weight. The pounds just poured off. In three days I went from a size 14 to a size 10. Bonnie Maurer, the daughter of my cousin Betty, who was a girl of Marianne's age, loaned me a cotton dress, which I wore for four days!

We took a three-bedroom townhouse at one of the Glick Company's properties, Williamsburg North on Sixty-second Street, just east of Allisonville Road, where Gene's dad already lived. Across the street and about a block away from the townhouse we also rented a two-bedroom apartment and used that as an office where I made phone calls and typed lists for the insurance claim. We had to document all that had been damaged or destroyed in the house along with details of the damage, and until I could do that, we could not start any reconstruction. People had to come over and do takeoffs of everything. Our insurance eventually covered everything lost in the fire, but Chubb refused to reinsure us after that.

On Tuesday I went downtown to L. S. Ayres to work with Jack Pomeroy, who had been the decorator for all our model apartments. He had furniture sent out right away, so we could move into the apartment as quickly as possible. The fire occurred on Sunday, and we moved into the townhouse and the other apartment Thursday.

It was close quarters. We had come from a house with five bathrooms. Marianne and Lynda had shared a bath, Gene and I had our own, and Arlene and Alice shared a bath. The live-in helper had her own bath. Additionally, there was our powder room adjacent to the master bedroom, where we had included a shower stall for added convenience. Now we were sharing one bathroom upstairs, with a half bath on the first floor. Marianne drove the girls out to get their own toiletries, toothbrushes, shampoo, cream rinse, and all of those items necessary for girls' survival. There were ten containers of shampoo and cream rinse lined up on the side of the only bathtub in this townhouse.

Gene could never stand to see a single hair in the bathroom bowl, so every time I walked by, I would take a Kleenex and wipe up any offensive hair. All of this was not easy.

School started. Marianne went back to Stephens. Somewhere along the line during this time just after the fire, my mother had a serious accident in the Borinstein Home. For years prior to this, I had talked to my mother about how nice it would be for her to go to that facility. She knew people over there and had been a volunteer there. When Odie left in the early 1960s, my mother was ready for the Borinstein Home. She moved into a second floor apartment where she was able to install some of her own furniture. A few years later she suffered a stroke and some memory loss. But one night in September, less than a month after the fire, when everything else was happening to me and my family, she fell off the commode and was taken to the hospital with a broken hip.

I did not want Mother to have an operation to set the hip, but the doctor, young Ed Steinmetz, said, "Mrs. Glick, your mother is in terrible pain. She needs to have this surgery." So we approved that, and for her recovery we hired round-the-clock private-duty nurses. Mother was in the hospital for one month. Some days I'd be awakened early in the morning by a call from Methodist Hospital advising, "The seven-to-three nurse didn't come today," and I'd go down there. Mother was more confused than she had been before. Sometimes I'd find her singing songs I'd never heard, undoubtedly tunes she had learned in her school days.

While my mother was in the hospital, we got a call from Stephens College. Marianne was not in school. She had disappeared. Her roommate had covered for her at night check for one or two nights, but then felt it was necessary to report her absence on the third day.

We surmised the truth. Gene flew to Boston and sure enough, he found Marianne with Allen. It was bad enough that she had left Stephens in this way, but we had to think about her future. Stephens was about to expel her with a negative report. I learned that if that happened, she couldn't get into another college ever again. Before Gene and Marianne returned to Indianapolis, I spent many hours on the phone with Stephens to be sure her records were completed to my satisfaction.

Marianne still wanted to marry Allen. It was at that time we talked to Allen's doctor, and he said, "Allen isn't ready to be married, and I have met your daughter. Frankly, she isn't ready to be married, either." Gene brought her back home.

Gene had scheduled a business trip to California in October and I had planned to go with him. I hated to leave while Mother was in the hospital. Still, she was to be released and return to the Borinstein Home the day after we were to leave. I hesitated, then called to get some input from Dr. Steinmetz. He told me, "Your mother may die at any time, or she could live for several years. You can't be with her every minute." I decided I could accompany Gene to California, and we left Tuesday. From the Beverly Hills Hilton Hotel I contacted the Borinstein Home to be sure my mother was back from the hospital and doing well.

I recall that after dinner on Saturday, as we walked into our hotel about midnight, the headline on the newspaper in the lobby was "Jackie

115

Marries Onassis." There was a phone message waiting for us from Indianapolis: "Your mother died." After surgery patients who remain immobile for a period of weeks are likely to develop blood clots. A fatal embolism had lodged in my mother's lung. Marianne was called to her bedside and was with her when she died.

We left for Indiana Sunday morning. Clarence and Sylvia Budd met us at the airport to drive us home. On Monday, Gene, Marianne, Arlene, Alice, and I flew to Detroit for a burial service at Clover Hill Park Cemetery, where Mother was placed next to my dad, as they had arranged many years before. Before we left Detroit, Sonia Duskin invited family and friends to lunch at her house.

Marianne was nineteen on November 25, 1968. Then she went back to Boston to spend some time with Allen and his family. Lo and behold, they decided to get married. The wedding was set for Saturday, January 4, 1969.

Marianne and Allen's wedding was to be a small one, just immediate family. When the day came, Allen's mother came to Indianapolis, along with his brother Joel and uncles and aunts. They slept on sleeping bags in the rented office apartment near our townhouse. The wedding took place in the small chapel at the temple, then we went to Broadmoor for dinner. Gene danced with Lynda, who was seven at the time.

Sunday we had a small brunch at Broadmoor, then Gene took the newlyweds out to the airport, while the rest of their family left later that afternoon. Our phone rang around midnight, awakening me from a sound sleep. Allen's brother Joel was calling from the airport in Indianapolis. There had been a terrible snowstorm in Boston and their plane could not land. He and his mother wanted to sleep once more in our other apartment. I left the key in the mailbox for them and went back to sleep. Late Monday afternoon they said goodbye again, and Gene drove them to the airport for the last time.

It had been just one thing after another, but more was to come. A week after the wedding, Gene was in the other apartment getting our golf bags into the car as we prepared to leave for our annual Dorado Beach vacation in Puerto Rico. The three girls and I were in the townhouse. Alice came down to tell me, "Arlene is in terrible pain." I went up and found Arlene in agony. I called Dr. Alex Kahn, who said, "Meet me at the hospital." We assumed she was suffering from appendicitis.

Arlene had surgery, and they discovered she had an ovarian cyst.

They removed this ovary and also took her appendix out while they were at it. I was concerned the removal of the ovary might affect Arlene's ability to have children, but the doctor said, "No, the other ovary will just take over." And that was apparently what happened, because after she was married, Arlene went on to have five children.

How fortunate it was that this incident occurred while we were still at home. Gene and I were about to depart for Puerto Rico, where we wouldn't have been able to handle this crisis or sign consent for Arlene's surgery without major complications. We postponed our golf trip since I needed to be with Arlene at the hospital and running the frantic schedule we had from the townhouse to the girls' schools each day.

Even before Arlene went into the hospital this schedule was difficult. Arlene and Alice were in high school, and I'd get up every morning and deliver the two older girls to North Central. Then I'd take Lynda back to the old neighborhood, so she could go on the school bus to Spring Mill School with Karen and Philip Larman. Karen was her closest friend, and she and Philip had played together since nursery school. Later in the day I'd pick up the girls from high school and then come back over to the old house and wait for Lynda's bus to drop her off.

While Arlene was in the hospital the schedule was further complicated. I came home from spending time at Methodist Hospital with Arlene on Friday evening to find that someone from the Glick Company had dropped off cases of liquor left over from the Christmas party to the townhouse where we were living. Where in the world was I going to put those cases in this crowded place? I broke down crying. Gene said: "You've got to find some place in the neighborhood where we can have some room, and so you don't have to do all that driving."

I began looking around. Soon my friend Joan Larman called me. She had been driving up the hill and noticed a For Sale sign in the nearby neighborhood. I took a look and it was perfect, giving us all the room we needed. We moved there on Monday, January 30, 1969.

Two days before that move, on January 28, I had another call from the Borinstein Home informing us that Aunt Sadie had passed away during the night. She had been living in the home for over a year. Her husband, Uncle Harry, had died before Gene and I were married.

So my mother died in mid-October, and now Aunt Sadie was gone three and a half months later, at age ninety. We arranged for her funeral and burial on Sunday at 10:30 a.m. at the IHC Kelly Street cemetery on the south side. That funeral was the end of a very bad chapter in my life.

The day after Aunt Sadie's funeral we moved into our substitute home and, as if by magic, the succession of trials and tribulations ended. Just as in the fairy tale, we "lived happily ever after." Once more we resumed our normal routines with plenty of space, close to friends and school. Our life became easier as Gene and I unraveled the complications of the restoration and rebuilding of our devastated house. It was impossible to find anyone willing to give us a firm bid on the demolition, but finally in the spring, Gene gave the job to John Kleinops and his crew. For seven weeks we watched the continuous procession of trucks headed for the dump with debris from our house. It would be March 1971, two and a half years later, before we could move back in.

Meanwhile, Allen and Marianne were taking up their life in Boston. As their plane was landing after the honeymoon, Allen told Marianne that he had been informed by his boss that he could have a week off to get married, but if he took more time than that, he would have to look for another job. So he was out of work. Eventually he got a job at Baskin Robbins. Marianne was not prepared to obtain a high-paying job either. She was able to get a temporary job doing simple tasks, typing insurance forms for instance, which bored her. She wanted to earn more money and also realized that she needed to complete her education. She was ready to go to college again.

Then Allen lost his job at Baskin Robbins because he failed to show up one morning. Clearly he was still growing up and trying to get a sense of responsibility, but in our eyes he was one of the family. He had such a winning personality; everybody loved him. By summer Marianne decided they would be better off in Indianapolis.

The Glick Company was developing an area of small homes out on Moeller Road on the west side of Indianapolis. The one-bedroom unit was very attractive, a little dollhouse of a home, and since all the one-bedroom homes were sold, the model was not going to be needed any more. Rather than selling, or renting it to someone else, we decided Marianne and Allen could live in this model. I went out and bought dishes, and they came back with their suitcases filled with pots and pans. In those days the airplanes were not crowded, so they put their TV set on a seat beside them.

They came in August with no car, so transportation was going to be a challenge. We arranged with Red Cab to provide cab tickets for Marianne so she could go to Marian College nearby.

Since we were still in the process of building houses in the Moeller Road project, Gene spoke to Kelly Lightle, the company's construction manager, and he arranged for Allen to join the crew as a carpenter. Allen did not need a car, since he lived so close to the job. One evening not long after the newlyweds had returned to Indiana, Marianne and Allen attended a Jewish Welfare Federation young couples' meeting. Each young man was asked to introduce himself, then introduce his wife, and tell about his occupation. Many of the young men were doctors or lawyers. Allen stood up to say, "I'm a carpenter." It embarrassed Marianne. One of the members of the group commented, "You must be the first Jewish carpenter since Jesus."

When Allen's mother came to visit and stayed with the couple, I invited her to be my guest for lunch. She came to the car toting a bag of run-down shoes. Neither Allen nor Marianne realized the simple fact that shoes had to be repaired. Marianne found that Allen couldn't take financial responsibility for their affairs, and she was running the house alone. They had a few litters of cats and their care of the cats and kittens left something to be desired.

Marianne persevered at college so that in three years she was ready to graduate and began student teaching. At the same time she realized she didn't want to be a teacher, she also realized she needed to leave Allen.

When Marianne came and told me she was divorcing Allen, I wasn't in favor of it. As far as I was concerned, marriage was a lifetime commitment. I had come to love Allen; he was a member of the family. It was very difficult, and Marianne didn't forgive me for a while because I was against this divorce.

I finally realized it wouldn't do any good for me to sit in the park for two hours crying over the split-up of this marriage and the loss of Allen. Marianne was coming out of her situation just fine and going forward. I would need to do the same.

Grandpa Glick loved his dog, Gretchen, and (l-r) Alice, Marianne, and Arlene—they all enjoyed being together.

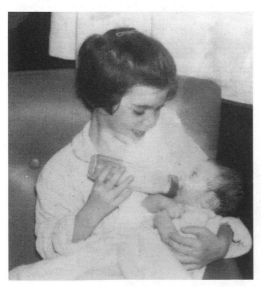

Calabash joined our family when Lynda was six years old.

Arlene feeds baby Lynda a bottle in our new house.

Even as a busy mother, from the earliest days I involved myself in civic causes. Here I'm with (l-r) Miriam Landman, Vivian Picar, and Pearl Jaffe.

The Guild was an important activity for me during the years with the girls at home. Here Pat Linderman and I wield shovels at the ground-breaking for a new building on Hoover Road. My good friend Marge Wolman is far right.

"Eugene — The Great"

Years ago, before we'd wed

I used to rub you on the head.

Then by the hour, I'd rub your back.

For massages — you did not lack.

Now through the years, we'd often wager

A rub down was the winner's pleasure.

Your mind is keener — you're always right

I must concede — I lose each fight.

So dear athlete of superior skill

Of rubbing you — I've had my fill!!

Unwrap this package — I've tied it loose.

Inside you'll find your new masseuse.

While president of Borinstein Home Guild, I told Gene I didn't believe I could leave for our annual golf trip in February, 1967. Reconsidering, I surprised him, bought tickets, and gave him this special card which entitled him to a professional massage.

North Group Membership Recruitment Chairman, Mrs. Eugene Glick (left) congratulates our 1000th member, Mrs. Max Beaty.

North Group Membership at 1000

by Donna Worth

North Group takes great pride in announcing that our membership is now one thousand strong! Membership Recruitment Chairman Mrs. Eugene (Marilyn) Glick deserves our congratulations' for her hard work in helping us achieve our goal. Our new members were honored at a spring brunch at the home of Mrs. Mel Simon on May 3. John Nelson, Indianapolis Symphony Orchestra Music Director, was the honored guest. With our many enthusiastic new members, we are hoping that next year will be our most successful and productive new year.

Our family gathers in our living room before the time of the fire.

1972. In our beautifully restored home after the fire.

*Marianne married
schoolmate Allen
Davis four months
after the fire.*

*Gene dancing with
Lynda at Marianne's
wedding.*

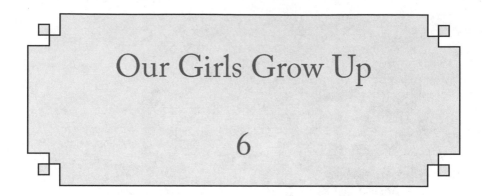

Our Girls Grow Up

6

When Arlene and Alice were teenagers, I was playing a lot of golf. I'd go to Broadmoor Country Club and play in the mornings with my friends, then in the afternoon, I would play another round with my girls as we pulled carts for eighteen holes. So I was playing thirty-six holes of golf daily all summer long. I spent a lot of time practicing, too. I was trying to lower my handicap and improve my game, but my handicap was never lower than twenty-four.

The first time I was ever on a golf course was in 1946 when Gene took me to Willowbrook par-three course. Except for ping pong, badminton and games in gym class in high school, I hadn't been exposed to playing sports as a young girl, so I had to learn golf as a beginner. Unlike tennis, golf does not come naturally, and developing an acceptable golf swing requires lots of lessons and many hours of practice.

Gene and I traveled out of state over a period of years to learn from the "pros" at six *Golf Digest* schools. In time I was satisfied enough with the way I played to participate in city tournaments and the Mayflower Classic.

A day before the official Ladies PGA tournament began, Mayflower moving company sponsored a benefit to raise money for various causes in the Indianapolis area. It was great fun and drew large crowds of spectators. Charitable amateurs played on each of eighteen teams headed by one of the lady pros, with each team consisting of four amateurs rated A-B-C-D. I was always the D player. Although I never hit the ball very far, my putting wasn't too bad, and I was able to help the team score on a few holes each year.

Golf had become our family sport, and I most enjoyed playing golf with my girls. They learned to play golf in Florida, where we took them for vacations at Christmas and in the spring. Since 1949 Gene and I had been taking lessons from George Valuck, who taught in West Palm Beach. When our little girls were in their formative years, they began learning to swing golf clubs from this exceptional teacher. Arlene was an apt pupil and was able to follow George's instructions quite easily. She practiced patiently while George was spending time with Gene and me. Although Marianne and Alice labored along through the one-hour lesson, it was Arlene who excelled.

When she was in high school, Arlene's handicap was good enough for her to join the eighteen-hole ladies' golf group at Broadmoor. She was soon playing the championship flight and was club champion five times. Gene used to quip, "From the way her parents play golf, you'd think we brought the wrong kid home from the hospital."

A young man named Tom Grande, who was working in the pro shop, watched Arlene as she teed off each afternoon and noticed she had a beautiful swing. He too loved to play golf, and after we walked off the eighteenth green with our pull carts one afternoon, he sauntered up to us and said to Arlene, "Would you like to play another nine?"

Arlene was having only a few dates, and I thought it would be good for her to spend time with this boy, so I said, "Go ahead, Arly, play another nine." They began to play a lot of golf. Afterward, he would bring her home in his car, such as it was. When the golf season was over, their friendship grew. The next summer I finally said, "Arlene, you're seeing an awful lot of Tom. Unless you are serious, you really shouldn't go on with him."

She replied, "Oh, I wouldn't marry Tom. He isn't Jewish."

Arlene and Tom both chose to attend Indiana University in Bloomington. Arlene decided in her junior year that she wanted to be a physical therapist and Tom was studying accounting. During college Arlene and Tom continued seeing each other and became inseparable. Halfway through that junior year at IU, she and Tom got engaged. They were both twenty years old.

I wasn't too happy about Arlene's marrying a boy whose parents were very staunch Catholics. Tom's father had studied to become a priest and frequently went to mass on his way home from work. I think his mother was always concerned that Tom would not go to heaven because he did not marry a Catholic girl and have the ritual of marriage performed in a traditional church. Still, because at that time in Indiana young men had to be twenty-one before they were eligible to marry, Tom's mother went down to sign the marriage license for him.

The rabbi at our temple would not marry Tom and Arlene. He sometimes made exceptions when a non-Jewish partner agreed to study Judaism and consider conversion. Tom was willing to study Judaism, but he was honest enough to say he would never convert. The rabbi would not even marry them in the outdoor chapel. Because our family had been dedicated to this temple from its early days, I was especially disappointed. Gene's grandfather Adolph Biccard had served as president of the Indianapolis Hebrew Congregation from 1916 to 1920. I thought this should have been considered.

I called all over the Midwest and could not find a rabbi who was willing to marry Arlene and Tom. We had planned the wedding for 2 p.m. on the afternoon of May 20, 1973. The Sunday wedding further complicated the arrangements, because rabbis were obligated to serve members of their own congregations on that day. In addition to helping children and staff at Sunday school, they were often required to conduct local funerals and weddings on Sunday.

One of the rabbis I contacted told me there was a chaplain at a hospital in St. Louis who would perform ceremonies under circumstances like ours. Since IHC was not available to us for this ceremony, we decided to have the wedding in our backyard. When the wedding day came, the weather was perfectly delightful. The three Sundays before that date and the Sunday after, it rained, so Tom and Arly were married with nature's blessing. We had planted magnificent azaleas in full bloom to enhance the beauty of the wide expanse of trees that defined our back property line. We worked hard creating a chuppah (wedding canopy), using the branches of a huge tree at the east end of our yard. My cousin, Betty Paller, helped me with this wedding and supervised the floral arrangement that was placed so artfully into the branches.

The chaplain did a marvelous job. I was surprised at how traditionally he conducted the ceremony, though I was fearful that the Grande family might have been uncomfortable when the rabbi raised his arms over the couple to say a priestly blessing in Hebrew. It would have bothered me to be in a church and have a priest chanting a blessing in Latin over my daughter's head.

Years later, when Arlene and Tom celebrated their twenty-seventh anniversary, they were married again in a special ceremony conducted jointly by a rabbi and a priest in a Catholic church. The Glick family and the Grandes enjoyed the ceremony, and I was pleased that the priest spoke in English throughout the entire service. Following the rites, we enjoyed being with all the Grande relatives at the celebration party. Hopefully Tom will be forgiven and find his way to heaven when he is no longer on this side of the grass.

Arlene's wedding gave us an opportunity to see old friends and family members. Through the years Gene and I stayed in touch with the Budd family, and Clarence and his wife attended the wedding. Clarence told me at that time he was thinking of retiring and asked my advice; I advised him that he should not retire. Just a few years after that, the government bought the building on Capitol Avenue. Clarence had a heart attack and died within two years after his retirement.

I wish I had been able to see Lester at the wedding, but he had died. Lester was handsome and charming and bright; he had graduated with honors from Butler. He had been the company salesman, calling on all the customers to buy the wipers the Budd Company made, and he must have done a wonderful job. Lester married Neoma Lichtenberg, and they had two sons, Marvin and Ronnie. Unfortunately Lester developed a malignant brain tumor and died young. We kept in touch with Neoma and invited her occasionally for Friday night family dinners. We attended her ninetieth birthday celebration at Beth-El synagogue, and she died less than a year later.

After the honeymoon, Arlene and Tom moved into a Glick apartment at Carriage House West, Phase IV, located near Tenth Street and Lynhurst Drive. Tom had planned to work and go to school at night. We wanted Tom to finish his education, so Gene presented him with a loan proposal that would allow him to go to Indiana University full time for the next year to earn his degree. If he completed his college work with a degree, Tom would not owe us anything at the end of that time. However, if he didn't finish college, he would be obligated to repay every penny of the loan we had advanced for his college education. Tom gladly accepted the proposal and drove to and from Bloomington each day to earn his degree in accounting within the next year.

Arlene took a year off from college when their daughter Jackie was born before the end of 1973. The following year she completed her physical therapy training at Home Hospital in Lafayette. When she graduated, they hired her to work for them in Lafayette, and Tom secured a position as an accounting supervisor with State Farm Insurance Company.

Three years later, when Arlene was about to have their second child, Michael, she left her job to devote herself to full-time motherhood. Then Tom had an opportunity to work for Union Federal Savings and Loan Company in Indianapolis. So the Grandes returned home.

They stayed with us a few weeks until they could move into the home they bought on Abbey Drive in Carmel. Tom worked as Assistant Controller for Union Federal for three and a half years. After he became a CPA, he was named Director of Accounting for Carnegie Life Insurance Company. When we decided to start involving ourselves in venture capital investments, Tom came to work for the Gene B. Glick Company as General Manager of Mount Vernon Venture Capital Company. During this time Tom attended Butler University at night and obtained a Masters of Business Administration Degree. He now works as Senior Vice President of Investments and Risk Management for the Glick company.

Their son Brian was born in 1979, daughter Laura in 1986, and Ben in 1991.

Arlene and Tom's five children were brought up in the Jewish faith. The children have all had Bar Mitzvahs or Bat Mitzvahs except Ben, who was involved in sports and didn't want to study Hebrew. He chose instead to be part of the confirmation class at IHC.

Meanwhile, Alice was following her own path. She was always a good student, though she rebelled a bit at homework assignments she considered repetitive or a waste of time. She was an original thinker who had no difficulty in solving problems on her own, often questioning with some indignation why she was assigned what she called "busy work." If you did one math problem correctly and understood the method, she questioned, why you should have to do twenty similar problems?

In the fourth grade Alice brought home a math test on which she had answered all questions correctly, but the teacher had given her a poor grade. She had not followed the steps outlined by her teacher to find each answer. I went over to school and told the teacher, "When I was in school, if you had the right answer on a test paper, it was marked correct."

The teacher said, "Well, Mrs. Glick, I will change the grade for you, but I think you are doing this child a great disservice." Her point was that the children were being taught to go through prescribed steps on the way to the answers. This lesson was designed to prepare the students for a world filled with computers.

As a child, Alice often shied away from social situations. I recall years later a friend invited her to a sweet sixteen luncheon at the Columbia Club. On the day of the party she said, "I wish I didn't have to go. I'm really more comfortable at home."

Alice graduated from North Central and went to Indiana University. Enjoying the life of a student, she signed up for both of the summer sessions each year. She would come home for only a few days and then go back one week early to get ready for the fall semester.

School had always come easy for her, and she made Phi Beta Kappa. "I don't think I'll join—they just want my money," she said. I told her that she should accept this honor which would enhance her resume when she entered the business world.

For graduate school, Alice considered Rutgers University, but decided to go to the University of Iowa. She thought she wanted to be a clinical psychologist, and Iowa had a reputation for having an exceptionally fine department in that field. Furthermore, this school offered her a scholarship that paid $4,000 a year and furnished her with an office.

In October she called me. "Mother," she said, "I don't want to be a clinical psychologist. I've found out what fascinates me. I want to be a computer programmer." The next semester she enrolled in computer science. So it seemed she could manage computers after all, even if she hadn't followed her fourth grade math teacher's instructions at Spring Mill Elementary School.

While Alice was free in Iowa for a few months, she took flying lessons. She never told me that when she soloed she'd crashed, smashing the wing on landing, a phenomenon known as a ground loop. She wasn't hurt, but she didn't fly much after that. Years later the girls told me she had taken Arlene up on one of her flights, and I had not known that either.

When Alice was in her second year of studying computer science, she felt she was prepared to work and wanted to get a job using her computer skills. I agreed, telling her, "I think after being in college for almost seven years, it would be good for you to be out in the real world." She got a job in Des Moines writing and maintaining computer programs for a magazine publishing company, staying with that job for a couple of years.

Toward the end of that time, she received a call from a headhunter in Detroit who wanted someone to set up computer programs for the automobile industry. When I went up with her to find an apartment, my cousin Marcia Diamond Lynn took us around, and Alice soon settled into a lovely apartment in Farmington Hills. Eventually Alice developed programs for almost every plant GM had in Detroit and the surrounding area.

Finally Alice realized she did not like the ice and snow of the upper Midwest. Florida would be better, she thought, and that is when she asked if she could live in our condo in Palm Beach. She moved and got a job with American Express. Alice's job was in Ft. Lauderdale, so for one year she commuted on I-95 from Palm Beach, an hour's drive each way five days a week.

During her second year in Florida, Alice rented an apartment in Boca Raton, just half an hour from Ft. Lauderdale. A few years later she decided it was time to find a husband and signed up with a dating service. That is how she met her husband, Andrew Meshbane. Andrew had been married before; his first wife was from a Russian refugee family. After their baby, Dora, was born, the couple divorced, and Andrew was awarded custody of Dora.

Alice and Andrew were to be married on January 27, 1985, in Palm Beach, so I stayed in Florida after the Christmas holidays to plan a lovely wedding. Alice selected her wedding dress without any help from me; then I had four weeks to make all the other arrangements. Like my own small wedding, only immediate family members of both sides were invited. I decided a 10:30 a.m. ceremony followed by a Sunday brunch would be appropriate and give those who needed to be at work the next morning more than enough time to fly home. I'd had plenty of experience after Arlene's wedding in 1973 and Marianne's three marriages (after Allen) during the years before this.

I was confident I could make all the arrangements required for this traditional Jewish wedding celebration. I engaged the rabbi of a conservative synagogue and bought the kiddush cup and candles from their gift shop. The volunteers I met there knew some of our Indiana friends. The owner-chef of a favorite restaurant of ours opened his small, elegant dining facility for this private party, though he was not otherwise open on Sundays. The flowers were magnificent and the wedding cake divine. I have to add I was proud and pleased that I had thought of everything. This wedding was complete and truly beautiful. The two families enjoyed meeting their new relatives, and we all had a very good time.

The following December Karyn was born. Now, with Karyn in the house, Dora had to share Alice's attention with the new baby, even though Alice was doing everything she could to make Dora feel loved. One day in February, while Alice and Dora were having lunch with Gene and me, I asked Dora, "How do you like your new baby sister?"

"Well," she answered, "I don't HATE her any more." How honest and perceptive for one so young. These two half-sisters accepted each other beautifully and got along very well as they were growing up. Alice knew enough psychology to let Dora make her own decisions. When Dora made mistakes as she was growing up, she had to pay the consequences if she needed to. In this way Dora learned the need to direct her own life. She and Alice got along without the struggle so many daughters and their mothers endure.

Dora has recently graduated from the School of Visual Arts in New York with a bachelor's degree in fine arts and has been doing some painting and working in a New Age store to support herself. Alice and Dora have a loving relationship, and I feel proud of both of them.

Alice finished courses at Florida Atlantic University to get her master's degree and then went on to get a doctorate in education. She has taught educational statistics, research, and measurement, and is currently self-employed as a data analyst. The family has a modest, but very comfortable four-bedroom house with a swimming pool and two dogs. Andrew loves to cook, so he does the cooking and Alice cleans up afterward. Not a bad arrangement!

Lynda was six years younger than Alice, and when Alice went to college, she would invite Lynda to Bloomington for the weekends. I'd go down to the Greyhound bus station and watch her get on the bus. Alice met her at the other end. On Sunday afternoons Gene and I would go down and meet Lynda on her return. She loved visiting IU and chose it for her own college education. However, she did not meet her husband at IU but rather at a Chanukah party for the youth group (United Synagogue Youth) of Beth-El Zedeck synagogue in Indianapolis. Their birthdays, coincidentally, were both September 12. Mark Schwartz is two years older than Lynda.

When Lynda and Mark decided to marry, I called the Hyatt Hotel to see if one of their large banquet rooms was available for the wedding reception. Gene said, "Why would you want to have the reception in a hotel when we have such a lovely backyard?" The answer was that I was concerned about the guest list. This could turn out to be a much larger wedding than Arlene's had been.

One hundred twenty-five people had attended Arlene's wedding. Lynda's list was much longer. Lynda is a perfectionist, and she wanted everything just so. It seemed as if we would have to hold the list for Lynda's reception to one hundred fifty if we held the wedding in our yard. Endless days throughout the summer I was out in the yard placing full sheets of newspaper I'd scotch-taped together to create ten-foot squares where fifteen tables and chairs might be placed for guests to comfortably dine at the reception. I was never satisfied with the arrangements.

Many people we knew expected to come, I guess. One acquaintance called wanting to know if she was on the wedding list. She was planning a trip, but said she would not go on the trip if she was to be invited!

The catering arrangements were getting complicated too. The backyard simply didn't seem to be the right spot. I called the Hyatt and found out they were still holding my date. That did it. Formal invitations had already been sent to 150 friends and family members, but I went to the Rytex stationery shop downtown, where I was thrilled to find fine quality stock immediately available. The shadowing of a beautifully artistic floral design accentuated this paper. I quickly drafted an invitation to be printed in burgundy ink on the pale pink background. In less than a week three hundred invitations were in the mail for the wedding that was held Saturday evening, August 21, 1982.

It was a gorgeous affair. The wedding at the Indianapolis Hebrew Congregation on North Meridian Street was beautiful in every way, and the Hyatt provided elegant ambiance and delicious food for the reception. The only problem was the photographer, who delayed the wedding party so very long taking pictures. It was about 10 o'clock when the catering staff served the buffet, offering a number of attractive stations. Later in the evening I was disappointed to notice a large group of guests leaving before the presentation of an elegant dessert station where guests could create their own sundaes.

Alice and Lynda had their babies about the same time. In December 1985 Karyn was born to Alice, and Jonathan to Lynda on January 8, 1986. Arlene thought it would be nice to have a baby to grow up with her sisters' children, and thus Laura Grande was born on May 30, 1986. It has worked out as Arlene had hoped. These cousins have enjoyed being together through the years at the Greenbrier resort hotel in West Virginia each summer and in Palm Beach each Christmas. Today they are very close, keeping in touch on the internet and getting together whenever they can.

Lynda has been a most devoted mother. When Jonathan was born one day after our thirty-ninth anniversary, Gene and I flew to California that morning. Jewish law prescribes that baby boys are circumcised on their eighth day in a ceremony known as a bris. I planned a party for the family and friends to celebrate this event, and I went out shopping for an extra tablecloth, items Lynda needed for the baby, food for the bris, and more. By the end of the day I had run up some $800-$900 worth of charges on my Visa card.

Edith, our cook, had come out to California with us, and I had filled five carts in the grocery store with the makings of the spread Edith would prepare to celebrate our family event. I gave the clerk at the checkout counter my charge card. Edith was heading out the door with a bag boy when the manager came out yelling, "Hold it. Don't take those carts out the door."

The store had been unable to get the charge approved. With so many out-of-state charges in one day, Visa operators were concerned this card might be stolen. Finally they did approve the charges, and we took the groceries to the car.

Meanwhile, Gene was busy looking at real estate along the freeway. The plan was that he would meet me at dinner. We were entertaining Lynda's husband's family, twelve of us, at Hemingway's on the ocean highway. When we finished our huge dinner and the bill arrived, they refused to honor our charge card. I had forgotten to tell Gene about the glitch at the grocery store.

He was angry with Indiana National Bank and almost cancelled our Visa card. We should have appreciated that the Visa agent was trying to protect their customer. It was necessary for Lynda's father-in-law to pay this large dinner tab. The bris went well. I was glad to be able to include two of my Koffman relatives who were residents of Leisure World in Laguna, not far from Lynda's home in Mission Viejo. One of Fanny Sachse's boys, Ernie, and his wife Tess were able to celebrate with us that day. Two and a half years later, when Lauren (Gigi) was born, I rented an apartment for Edith for a full month.

During these years Gene's dad was always an integral part of family gatherings, and we spent a considerable amount of time together. Our girls were lucky to have such a grandfather. He was like Santa Claus, jovial, warm, and loving with a full shock of white hair. In fact, for many years, until he was 85, he played Santa Claus at the Elks Club on a Saturday afternoon. The next day, wearing his costume, he would come and visit all of the children in our neighborhood.

He was still active through his early eighties, though he had developed diabetes in his mid-fifties. The winter he was eighty-four, he drove his car to Florida and enjoyed it. Not long after his eighty-fifth birthday, he spent five weeks in the hospital, and that's when we decided he should spend all his winters in Florida. We tried to arrange for the private-duty nurse who had taken care of him in the hospital to be with him in Florida.

I don't believe his nurse really ever wanted to go with Grandpa, but she said she would be willing if she could bring Lamb Chop, her Great Dane. Gene and I made a special trip to Florida looking for an available rental where they could bring two dogs. Gene had given his dad a dachshund after his mother's death and Grandpa loved that dog. Lamb Chop and the nurse did not end up going to Florida, but fortunately we had been able to rent a house and hired Mary Miley, a wonderful assistant, who was with Grandpa for over ten years until he died in April 1980.

My interest in service to the community continued through these years as the girls grew up and married.

I had become chairman of the Hooverwood Guild raffle, a modest project that raised about $3,000 or $4,000 a year. Previously, they had sold dollar tickets. Many people were satisfied to buy individual tickets, while my friends and I felt generous when we bought two or three of their books of ten tickets. After the first year I eliminated the dollar tickets; they just didn't pay.

Then I went through a set of computer punch cards created by the Jewish Welfare Federation. Those who never gave to the JWF were not solicited. The rest of the prospects were sent a mass mailing, which included a return envelope addressed to Hooverwood Guild and an order form for ten dollar tickets. The response was good.

For years Lucille Cohen was my co-chairman, and together we organized a large committee of our friends and guild members. Lucille hosted our kick-off luncheons, where each guest was assigned ten books of tickets to buy or sell. I created long sheets listing every ticket to record these assignments as well as all our sales and donors. We drafted men and women for two nights of phone-a-thons at Gene's office in Indianapolis, using the phones to ask people to buy raffle tickets and taking orders for close to $10,000 worth of tickets each night. Twenty-five of us would gather at the office. We'd serve a light supper, and then we'd go to the desks where stacks of twenty-five cards were placed by each phone together with instructions for the brief solicitation. At the end of the evening, form letters and envelopes were waiting to be completed by our volunteers. The appropriate tickets were enclosed and prepared for mailing to all who had placed orders. These contributors were to fill out their stubs and return them with a check in the envelope, which was already addressed to the guild.

Together Lucille and I worked diligently all summer selling books. We appreciated our members' generosity. Eventually we brought our profits from the raffle up to $44,000 a year. Later and in recent years my friends Joan Larman and Helaine Simon have chaired this important committee, together with a very dedicated team of workers who usually succeed in raising a like sum of money each year. These funds have been used to purchase many unbudgeted necessities for Hooverwood, including at least two special wheelchair-accessible vans, special electric therapy beds, and an automatic electronic door at the front entrance to assist residents using wheelchairs and walkers.

Why is it that I enjoyed all this community involvement? Many people join groups to make friends. I have made a lot of friends whom I've come to know well in community service groups, but making acquaintances was not my objective, except when I was a teenager! As a married woman, if I wanted to be with friends, I could have gone to play cards.

I'm not alone in my deep devotion to civic causes, but not everyone is willing to put in as much time as I have. I really enjoy the challenge of this work, but I think I create unnecessary stress when I so often make this work a priority. Then I get behind in personal business at my desk, sometimes neglecting my dearest friends. I am ashamed at how bad I am about sending thank-you notes.

The Gene and Marilyn Glick Foundation was established in 1983. I was busy with family, friends, and my work with various organizations, leaving the management of the foundation to Gene in the early days. However, I was interested in many of the projects we began supporting. One of the first projects we established over twenty-five years ago was our PRO-100 program. This unique undertaking provides training and opportunity for inner-city high school youth. It was established by Gene before the foundation began, in 1981, through private and public funding. Disadvantaged youth applied and were interviewed and hired to work at public schools and, in those days, public golf courses, painting, planting, and beautifying these facilities while learning employment skills. They earned minimum wages and during their lunch hour the teenagers were taught how to prepare and present themselves for a job interview. At the end of the summer, students also received high school credit for this seven or eight week program. It was particularly satisfying to me to see this program in action because I believed it made a real difference for teenagers who otherwise might be at risk for behavior which could get them into trouble.

As the years have evolved, we have taken advantage of various "naming" opportunities with the charities we support. In this way we have been able to honor deceased loved ones who had a special interest in the work of these particular charities.

I believe, as the scriptures say, "for everything there is a season." As is true in the lives of most people, Gene and I have experienced some periods I might have felt were the "worst of times." But compared to the ordeals most of the people on this earth suffer, our difficulties have been insignificant. Most of our lives we have been blessed with the "best of times." In gratitude I hope we are making wise choices as we attempt to contribute to our community. Perhaps we can make a difference. At least we are trying.

Golf seems to be a constant in the life of our family. Devoted friends Joan and Leonard Larman formed a persistent golf foursome with us. Here we are in 1973.

Arlene and I played this Pro-Am round with an LPGA pro and two amateur golfers.

Ruby loved playing Santa. Next to Gene are Philip Larman in front of Alice. That's Lynda licking on her candy cane.

The bartender, Herb Howard, lights candles on Grandpa's birthday cake as Arlene, Grandpa, Alice, and Marianne look on. My back is to the camera.

Arlene is escorted by Gene to the altar on her wedding day, May 20, 1973.

Family in the garden at Arlene's wedding (l-r) Marianne, Gene, Marilyn, Arlene, Tom, Alice, Lynda and Grandpa.

Jackie and Michael herald the approach of the bride at Lynda's wedding as flower girl and ring bearer.

Lynda and Mark are at the altar.

Lynda's wedding, bridesmaids (l–r) Martha Levensen, Arlene, Alice, Marilyn, Lynda, Gene, and to the right Sharon Ossip, Karen Larman, and Marianne.

(l–r) Sylvia Budd, Neoma Budd, Rose Schiller, and Helen Dushkin visit at Lynda's reception.

(l–r) Chuck Isaacson, Faye Dushkin Isaacson, Murray Jacobs, and Sonia Dushkin Jacobs at Lynda's wedding reception.

Lynda's and Mark's wedding 1982: my cousins Donald and Maxine Schiller and our friends Bud and Dorothy Gerson.

Gene and Alice on their way to her wedding.

Alice's wedding with Alex, Amelia, and Andrew Meshbane, Alice, Marilyn and Gene.

Five year old Brian Grande thought no one would notice if he had an early taste of frosting off the wedding cake that day.

Our first grandchildren, Jackie and Mike Grande.

*Grandma and Grandpa happily present Ben Grande his
first set of golf clubs.*

Jonathan Schwartz with Laura Grande outside our Florida condo December 1987.

Jonathan's sister, Lauren Schwartz, at eight and a half months.

Dora and Karyn became true sisters over the years.

Laura Grande, Karyn Meshbane, and Jonathan Schwartz were born less than six months apart.

(Clockwise) Joan Lanman, Inda Singer, Loretta Marra, and I at Highland Country Club. It's 18-hole Guest Day.

Museum Of Art Chair: Many Civic Roles

November 14, 1980 The Jewish Post and Opinion Page 18

"It's a way of life for me. I love serving the community by doing volunteer work," said Mrs. Marilyn Glick reflecting on her appointment as chair of the residence phase for the Indianapolis Museum of Art 1981 Operating Fund Campaign.

Although this is her first year in this position, Mrs. Glick has been an active participant in the Operating Fund for ten years. She has served as a special gifts worker, captain, division leader and Phone-A-Thon volunteer.

"MY INVOLVEMENT with the museum springs from my appreciation of the tremendous asset our museum is to this community. I enjoy the Art Study Group sponsored by the IMA Alliance and have been membership chair for the Contemporary Arts Society," she said.

Support raised during the campaign makes possible the wide variety of exhibitions and programs as well as the day-to-day operating functions of the museum. Additionally, the Operating Fund has kept the museum's permanent collection open to the public with no admission charge. It's one of the last major museums that does not charge at the door.

"Because of the tangible evidence of service to the community, it's easier to encourage membership. The

MRS. MARILYN GLICK
...community leader

museum is a business investment for Hoosiers because company executives are more interested in relocating to a city that has strong cultural activities." she states.

OUT-OF-TOWN visitors to the home of Eugene and Marilyn Glick will find themselves at the museum or one of the other many arts events or attractions within the metropolitan area and throughout the state.

How and why did this active community service begin?

"I learned at an early age from my parents, primarily from my father, how much fun working for the community can be and the rewards it brings," she said.

Her father, a devoted civic leader in Detroit, was active in the Masonic Lodge, B'nai

B'rith, Sharrey Zedeck Congregation, Zionist Organization of America, and the Jewish National Fund.

Mrs. Glick's first experience in fundraising came when she was just seven years old. She solicited for the JNF Flower Day in Detroit and raised the most money.

AFTER her father's death when she was 11, she became active in the junior congregation at Shaarey Zedeck and enjoyed delivering sermonettes on the sedra or the haftorah, a major honor given to the junior congregation once or twice a year, she explains.

Her mother returned to Indianapolis where her family lived, and Marilyn completed high school at Shortridge. She became active in the Indianapolis Hebrew Congregation and taught Sunday School at Beth-El Zedeck Congregation.

Mrs. Glick continued her education at Indianapolis Business College and following her marriage, she and her husband began building the Eugene B. Glick companies, and during that time she earned her realtor's license.

WHAT, does she feel, is her greatest accomplishment?

"That's easy to answer," she claims.

"Our four daughters."

Gene and I supported the arts for many years. In 2003 we received the Indiana Governor's Arts Award for our contribution to the arts community.

Collecting Art

7

Let me go back, briefly, in this story to that time just after the fire. A chance event encouraged my interest in art, an interest that would flourish in years to come. I was on my way home from shopping downtown for much needed clothing just five days after the fire when I decided to stop and look inside the Herron Art School and museum on the corner of Sixteenth and Pennsylvania. That day, September 2, 1968, I made my first purchase of art, a little metal sculpture, for $100.

Perhaps it was euphoria, a feeling of relief and freedom from the anxiety and stress of the past five days, that caused me to make a detour into the art museum. On that day I had no awareness that art would become such a major interest in my life. In fact, in the days and months that were to follow, I had no time to focus on anything but the needs of the moment: paperwork for insurance, supervision of restoration of the house, driving our children to two schools each day, and facing one crisis after another. Life did improve considerably when we were able to buy a home nearby, where we lived comfortably until we moved back into our reconstructed home. It was only then that I was once more truly free to pursue what must have been a latent love of art.

Now as I look back, I believe my appreciation of the arts was always a part of my life. You may recall that as a baby I loved hearing my mother sing while she tried to rock me to sleep. I imagined a world of my own, looking over her shoulder at Bonet's *Girl at the Fountain*. Later, before I went to kindergarten, I was awed at the Detroit Institute of Arts, where my parents took me to see the unveiling of Diego Rivera's murals depicting auto workers toiling on factory assembly lines. And how I loved going to Belle Isle with Aunt Sadie and Uncle Harry to hear symphony concerts in that enormous park.

The summer before I left Detroit, I spent glorious summer days with my friend, Miriam Weisman (now Butzel), listening to classical records in her home on Boston Boulevard. During my dating years I especially liked boys who took me to plays and concerts. A highlight was the night my date took me to hear Leonard Bernstein as he appeared under the stars in Indianapolis. While we dated Gene and I shared symphony concerts and "Evenings with Sigmund Romberg" at the Murat Temple, and shortly after we were married, we bought season tickets for the Indianapolis Symphony Orchestra. We continued our support and enjoyment of the symphony after the orchestra moved to Clowes Hall. When the orchestra completed renovation of the Circle Theatre, Gene and I went down to choose our seats for the classical concerts we attend.

I was interested in the visual arts as well and joined an art study group founded in the early 1970s, but this hadn't motivated me to purchase any art for our home. I had been perfectly satisfied with what I already had from my mother's home and from the Glicks.

Let me tell you how our business created opportunities for me to begin buying art. In the early years the Glick Company had occupied a number of offices scattered throughout various projects on the east side of Indianapolis. By 1971 most of the employees had moved to a relatively small office complex at Eighty-sixth Street and Guilford Avenue. The company was in that location for less than five years. Then, with a steadily increasing volume of building, there was a need to consolidate the growing staff into one office. So in 1975 the Gene B. Glick Company moved into new offices at Ninety-first and Meridian streets. It was the first time all of our Indianapolis employees were together in one office building.

The new facility had work stations, lots of partitions to divide offices, and long corridors with nothing but gray walls. I thought the office needed some art and color to create interest and break up the monotony. To beautify that office I began buying colorful photocopies of great work by well-known artists.

By this time the Art Association of Indianapolis, which operated John Herron School of Art, had become the sponsoring group of the Indianapolis Museum of Art and had moved to the beautiful and spacious grounds of the former J.K. Lilly estate at Thirty-eighth Street and Michigan Road. Among the many new amenities and services was a rental gallery located on the main floor of the museum. After renting a piece for a month or two, a patron could buy it, with the rental fees applying to the total purchase price. I bought a lot of art at the museum rental gallery for the office and for our home.

It was so convenient to pick up wonderful works by Indiana artists, which I enjoyed having in my home as well as in the Glick offices. I credit the IMA for leading me into collecting art. I believe it is unfortunate that this rental service is no longer available at our beautiful new museum building. I know of no other co-op or commercial gallery offering a rental service with option to buy.

Later, when I became interested in fine art, I asked the then museum director Robert Yassin and contemporary art curator Holly Day for help in selecting pieces to beautify our home. "How should I select art for our home? What should I buy?" I wanted to know. Their advice was: "Only buy good art." Their answer was an enigma to me. How was I to recognize good art?

"Just look at lots of art and you will know," they insisted. Following their advice, gradually I began to find pieces of art that called to me.

As I drove through Broad Ripple on my way to the Glendale Shopping Mall, I frequently passed Editions Limited, then located on Westfield Boulevard, between Guilford and Winthrop avenues. I had never before paid much attention to art galleries. Since I was now looking at "lots of art," however, I began stopping in this gallery often. Editions Limited displayed a wide variety of art, including good pieces by local artists as well as work by nationally known artists that were priced accordingly. It was a good place to experience lots of art. I was able to select limited edition prints and a few originals for both our home and the office. During this time I was also visiting local co-op galleries, one-person shows, and the Hoosier Salon.

After I became more experienced, I might ask a gallery owner to hold a piece for me while I considered it, then frequently return to make the purchase. Still, I was hesitant about spending a lot of money just because I liked a piece. The only regrets I have now are for some fine pieces I loved but was afraid were beyond my means. It was a long time before I was confident enough in my own judgment to spend more than a few hundred dollars on any one piece of art.

So I purchased a lot of inexpensive art for the office during this period. I began stopping often at the Art League (now the Indianapolis Art Center) in the small house they occupied in those days on Sixty-seventh

Street just east of College Avenue. In the 1970s I made purchase prizes at their annual shows each May to encourage Indiana artists. At one of those shows I bought a large piece, *He Brings Botecelli's Venus Home.* I took this piece to the office and said to a secretary there, "Would you like to have this picture here?" She declined, no doubt embarrassed to have opposite her desk that canvas depicting a naked Venus confronting a suburban family in their living room. No one in the office wanted it, so I put it into the public restroom on our floor. When we moved the office ten years later, I took this charming canvas to our house, where it is a great conversation piece for the groups who come to tour our collection.

Another piece by this artist used this same family (his own, I presume). In this work, the same characters are in the family van. The man is driving while a St. Christopher medal dangles from the rearview mirror. His wife is nagging, the dog barking, the children fighting and all are disgruntled. This one is titled *On the Way to Bear Mountain for a Week's Vacation.* It is still enjoyed by our employees at the company office.

My exposure to, and judgment about, quality in works of art was growing. The more I collected, the more interested I became in having better art in our home to add to those pieces I had from my mother and Gene's mother.

I bought art in other cities, too. And I liked to accompany Gene when he traveled to New York. The Gene B. Glick Company had completed its program of building National homes. By the 80s the company had constructed apartment projects in fourteen states, with an emphasis on subsidized housing under HUD programs.

Favorable financing had always been part of the company's management strategy, so Gene frequently visited lenders on Wall Street. I liked to travel with him for these three or four day trips, and in the evenings we took in shows on Broadway. Before I became so interested in art, I would shop for clothes, but later I visited the famous museums and art galleries so readily available in the city. In New York I found appealing works of art for our home, and some of these eventually made their way into our office.

Now the need to have work by well-known contemporary artists was growing stronger. I had become actively involved in the Contemporary Art Society of the IMA (Indianapolis Museum of Art.) For a while I served as membership chairman. Another year during this time I was on the selection committee for the museum's biannual contemporary art show. I went to New York with Gene ahead of the committee that year and visited the galleries on their list to make my recommendations. Later I traveled to Chicago with the group as we completed the selection process for the upcoming contemporary art show in the spring.

In the fall of 1982 a whole new art medium began to consume me.

Although I had developed and refined my own interest in art as I've described through the 1970s with the purchase of works in acrylics, pastels, watercolors, prints, metals, and wools and other fabrics, along with wood and clay, I had never focused on any one specific medium.

Suddenly that changed. In October 1982 a glass show opened at Ann Kaplan's Artifacts Gallery in Broad Ripple. The star of the show was a piece I liked, but it was $1,200 and the artist was unknown to me. I ended up purchasing a Sylvia Vigiletti instead, a small "veiling piece," clear glass enclosing a metallic layer.

On October 6, 1982, a Van Gogh show also opened in Toledo. My friend and neighbor Joan Larman was interested in art. We both wanted to see this show and made arrangements to visit girlhood friends living in Detroit a day before going to Toledo. I spent the night with my closest friend, Dorothy (Davidson) Gerson, and Joan arranged to spend the night with her friend from early days, Carol Margolis, who was married to Henry Frank, a trustee of the Detroit Institute of Arts.

Dorothy had a tall cabinet in her living room filled with glass, including some fine Lalique once treasured in her childhood home. She had also bought contemporary glass by this time and told me about her exceptional pieces of contemporary studio glass by already well-known American artists Dale Chihuly, Harvey Littleton, and Joel Philip Myers. All this art was displayed in that one glass cabinet. I admired those very beautiful works, just as I have always admired Dorothy. This visit encouraged me to become interested in glass.

Ten years earlier I had spent a day visiting Lu (Lucretia) Osterman, who had moved from Indianapolis to Toledo. After visiting most of her favorite places, the two of us had lunch at the Toledo Museum of Art, where glass was displayed in a large gallery. I was impressed by their Depression glass. I remembered in the early thirties many of the gas stations thanked customers who filled their tanks with a gift of this cheap glass. Now it has appreciated and can be purchased by collectors at antique shows.

Since Ohio was the home of Johns Manville glass company (which had bought Libby Owens Ford glass company), it was appropriate for this museum to devote considerable space to a glass gallery. As we were leaving the museum, Lu told me, "There is a wonderful glass artist you would love, but we don't have enough time to see him. My daughter will be home from school soon and I have to be back by 3. But next time you come, you must see him."

Now, in October 1982, when I was attending the Van Gogh show, I asked several people who was the "wonderful glass artist" I should be seeing from this area, the one my friend Lu had talked about during my earlier visit. Lu wasn't in Toledo that week, and nobody seemed to know to whom she'd been referring. It was in fact Dominick Labino, one of the great pioneers of the studio glass movement, though I did not know it. The reason no one had the answer for me is that this artist lived in a farmhouse over an hour's drive from Toledo.

On the weekend after my 1982 Toledo trip, Gene and I traveled to Florida and spent the weekend in our condo in Palm Beach. In those days when I spent time in Palm Beach, I never missed a day on Worth Avenue. I loved the architecture of buildings designed by the Addison brothers, and it was a joy to stroll off the avenue down Via Mizner and all the other charming lanes filled with a myriad of small shops displaying designer wear and lots of art, both contemporary and antique. Worth Avenue was a shopper's paradise.

Our daughter Alice had recently told me about Holsten Gallery on the avenue, devoted exclusively to contemporary glass. So on that Saturday I stepped into Holsten and discovered they were featuring a show of sculpture by Harvey Littleton, the artist whose beautiful glass work Dorothy had shown me in her home only a few days earlier. I recognized Harvey Littleton's name, and now knew that he was important in the studio glass movement.

Since I am kinetic by nature, it is no wonder I was fascinated by the Littleton "rocking piece," which was molded into an inverted "C." The piece was balanced on a clear glass block, and when touched very lightly, the sculpture would rock for almost five minutes.

"I love that piece," I told the dealer, "but I want my husband to approve it. Would you please bring it out to our apartment, just ten minutes away, so my husband can see it? " It was more money than I had paid for anything before. Not wanting to miss a sale, Kenn Holsten agreed. Gene did like the piece, and I told Mr. Holsten to hold it for me.

On Monday morning "back home in Indiana," I called Bob Yassin at the art museum and asked him about the piece. "After all," I thought, "glass is a fragile material." I was concerned about investing a good sum of money in something that might crack or break. Bob assured me that Littleton's glass sculpture would not be easily broken, would hold its value, and would be a fine piece for me to buy. This was encouraging.

Next I called Penelope Steibel at the Metropolitan Museum of Art in New York City, because she was the author of an article I'd just read in the Holsten gallery on Saturday. I had a long conversation with her, telling her of my concern about putting money into a piece of glass that might prove breakable. She assured me it was a substantial art form, not overly fragile.

She went on to tell me that Littleton and Dominick Labino had together founded the Studio Glass movement. Littleton was born in Corning, New York, into a glass-making family (the senior Littleton had invented Pyrex) and as a child Harvey had spent a good deal of time among people designing and manufacturing glass.

After service in World War II and training in art in America and abroad, Littleton was teaching ceramics at the University of Wisconsin. He had a dream that glass could be crafted in a studio environment (as opposed to a factory setting) by artists who would design and fire glass into sculptures, attending personally to the entire production from start to finish. Littleton believed that one day those who appreciated art in other media might come to buy unique glass sculptures created by artists in their private studios.

Littleton resented his father because his "old man" believed the son's dream of creating works of glass art in a studio was a crackpot idea. But he was determined to pursue his dream.

Through his Corning connections, Littleton knew the director of the Toledo Museum of Art, who gave him permission to conduct experiments in an empty building adjacent to the museum. In 1962 he invited local and neighboring artists working in clay to participate.

Dominick Labino was the chief chemist at Johns Manville fiberglass manufacturing company. His position in Ohio was identical to the position held by Harvey Littleton's father at Corning in New York. It is not at all surprising that the younger Littleton should have invited Labino to his workshop in Toledo. In the beginning these two men were credited with being the fathers of the Contemporary Studio Glass Movement.

It was in this first workshop that formulas were devised and ingredients mixed as these artists attempted to create glass pots and vessels in an intimate setting, a revolutionary idea in glassmaking. The pieces were then fired in the furnace Littleton himself had made.

Labino was the chemist responsible for working color into the glass in these first attempts. When he and Littleton failed during the first day of the workshop to get color into their glass vessels, Labino returned home and melted some marbles. It was because of Labino's important chemical contribution to the success of the next day's experiments that Harvey Littleton and Dominick Labino came to be regarded as the founding fathers of contemporary studio glass. After more experiments, Littleton was able to convince the art department at the University of Wisconsin to let him teach glassblowing. Soon Littleton and Labino began to visit other universities, encouraging them to introduce glassblowing into their art curricula. Littleton himself became a renowned teacher of studio glass art.

For the rest of his life, Labino continued serving as Vice President and Director of Research at Johns Manville. But at his farmhouse he continued experimenting with color in glass and was a highly regarded glass artist. Littleton went on to become one of the most collected and valued artists in the movement he had helped to create.

Before I ended my conversation with Penelope Steibel, she had given me Harvey Littleton's phone number. Within a short time I made three calls to him to discuss my interest in the rocking piece. We became friends over the phone and he helped me make my decision.

Penelope also gave me the names of two other galleries carrying rocking pieces by Harvey Littleton. One gallery she recommended was Heller Gallery in New York. When I called Heller, they sent out transparencies of a piece which was more colorful but not as graceful as the one I was considering at the Worth Avenue gallery. On Steibel's recommendation I also called Habatat Gallery in Detroit. Their Littleton rocking piece was about a thousand dollars less, so I asked this gallery to send me a picture as well.

Then I asked Holsten to send his Littleton rocking piece on approval to my home in Indianapolis.

By this time my friend Lucretia Osterman was back in Toledo. I called her to ask the name of the glass artist she had wanted me to see ten years earlier. When she told me his name was Dominick Labino, whose name and story I now knew well, I got in touch with Labino immediately and made arrangements to visit him with Lu the next Monday.

I returned for a third time to Toledo, and Lu picked me up at the airport. Then we headed out to Labino's farmhouse. There I was thrilled to acquire a fine example from his signature series titled *Emergence*.

Tom McGlaughlin was another artist living in Toledo who had attended Littleton's workshop in 1962 and was now teaching glassblowing in Toledo. He created the piece I had so admired at Ann Kaplan's gallery in Broad Ripple. I made an appointment to see him after our Labino visit. McGlaughlin had fourteen of these vessels in his home. I was surprised to find he was asking $200 more for each of them than Ann Kaplan was charging for the similar piece she was offering. What's more, I really liked the piece in Indianapolis better than any of his work in Toledo! So I made my decision in favor of the piece at Artifacts.

The next morning Lu and I returned to the Toledo Museum, where I bought five pieces of contemporary glass from the craft shop: four paperweights and a small vessel by Meredith Wenzel, one of McGlaughlin's students. I also bought three paperweights by Leon Applebaum, who was an artist no longer living in Toledo.

From there we drove to Detroit to see the Littleton rocking piece that Habatat was offering for sale. I didn't think it was nearly as interesting and colorful as the one from Holsten Gallery now in my home on approval. I was pleased, however, that Habatat was featuring a Dale Chihuly show just then, and I bought a spectacular machia basket. It is now on display at the IMA and is one of Barry Shifman's favorite pieces. Barry was Curator of Decorative Art at the Indianapolis Museum of Art for sixteen years. During half of that time, we worked together building the glass collection for the museum. He had wanted to move on after the turn of the century and left our museum in July 2007 for a position with the Virginia Museum of Fine Arts in Richmond. I am glad to know he is happy now that he is so close to Washington, D.C.

In the fall of 1982, when I returned from that most recent trip to Toledo, there was no doubt about the purchase of the rocking piece from Holsten Gallery on Worth Avenue. Harvey Littleton had told me I would be happier with the "inverted C" than any of the other pieces I was considering, and he was right.

Suddenly I realized I had bought ten pieces of contemporary studio glass in just two weeks. They included the Labino piece, the Chihuly machia basket, four paperweights, the Wenzel piece, the Littleton "inverted C," and both the small piece with veiling on it by Sylvia Vigelenti and McGlaughin's vessel from Artifacts Gallery.

I had become hooked on contemporary glass art. It soon became an addiction. The more I learned and saw, the more I admired these spectacular pieces. In the beginning I bought only the beautiful works I wanted for our home. For me glass art encompasses the magic reflection of light, and that essence enchants me. Glass filters and transmits light and emphasizes surface variants, texture, and color. Each piece I chose had to satisfy my aesthetic sense. I really don't think I chose glass; I think glass chose me.

The day I bought that machia basket at Habatat, they gave me a small booklet entitled "14 glass artists." A picture of Mark Peiser's *Lilies of the Valley* grabbed my attention. We had a patch of delicate lilies of the valley growing in our backyard on Hazelwood and Second in Detroit. I fell in love with this vase made like a paperweight. I contacted many glass galleries but Peiser's paperweight vessels were not available anywhere. Peiser had moved on to casting his work. Twelve years later at an auction of early work, I was able to buy *Lilies of the Valley*.

In those early days, when I made a purchase, the gallery would give me catalogues or booklets in hopes of making a sale or developing me as a regular customer. The owner would later follow up with some tempting photos or transparencies. And with some phone encouragement, the next step would be to send the work out on approval. If I decided to keep the piece there was no delivery charge, but if I wished to return the piece it was at my expense. It was easier for me than taking a plane to see all this glass.

There really were no collectors at that time in Indianapolis, with the exception of one man, Dr. Hanus Grosz, who included glass in his large and varied art collection. So I may have been the first real collector of contemporary studio glass in Indianapolis. If so, that did not happen by design. I had no intention of being a collector. It was by now an addiction full of personal delight for me.

I liked the fact that I did not have to consult Gene, though I would ask his opinion from time to time. Most of the glass collectors I know are couples, and they collect contemporary glass as a hobby. Each of them must agree on a piece before they add it to their collection. In my case, I was the person who decided. I was free to make my own selections.

By 1988 I had collected over two hundred pieces from major glass artists in the country, including several Littletons and Labinos as well as Chihulys and Peisers and Lipofskys. I took a particular interest in the latter two while buying eighteen pieces by Joel Philip Myers.

As far as Peiser goes, I found one of the finest pieces of my collection in late June of 1984, when I discovered the most beautiful paperweight vessel on Madison Avenue at Heller Gallery in New York. It was in the lower level where consignment pieces were displayed. I believe this is one of Mark Peiser's best paperweight vessels and certainly the most interesting. I have had so much pleasure in our home with this piece, displaying it on a turntable. I tell my guests about it in this way:

"It is summertime," I say, turning the piece on the turntable, "and we see the gold of the sun, and then the trees, followed by storm clouds and next the bubbles resembling rain. By this time we have gone full circle and are back to summertime." However, when we placed this vessel among seventy-five pieces in the special IMA show of a major part of the collection in 1997, commemorating our fiftieth wedding anniversary, Barry Shifman contacted Mark Peiser, to verify the title. The artist called it *The Wheat Piece*.

When I bought the Peiser piece at the Heller Gallery, the owner gave me another catalogue, from the Lever Brothers show of 1978. An illustration of an outstanding Marvin Lipofsky two-part sculpture appeared in this booklet, and I was smitten. Because I could not find his work in any of the galleries I visited, I managed to get his home phone number in Berkeley, California. He had a very volatile personality and had trouble getting along with the galleries. If a gallery owner sold a piece of his and did not send him the money right away, he would call and berate the owner. Personal relationships with Lipofsky became such a problem that gallery owners did not want to bother with him, so he wasn't in many galleries. It took me almost a year of letters and phone calls to Marvin Lipofsky and to Kenn Holsten on Worth Avenue to arrange for them to get together. I was hoping Holsten would accept Lipofsky's work so that when I was in Florida I might have an opportunity to select some work of this talented artist.

They finally agreed on terms, and Lipofsky sent five pieces to Palm Beach. After I went down to see them I was happy to buy one of his California series. In appreciation of my having facilitated their getting together, Kenn Holsten gave me a sizeable discount on this one piece.

Several months later I went to California to visit Dolly Falender, who had moved to the Golden State in the 1960s. Her home was not far from Berkeley. So we made an appointment to visit Lipofsky. At his home I bought a two-part piece from his California Storm series. Hanging on the wall was a framed picture of the piece I had bought from Holsten three months earlier. I wanted this picture, too, but he did not wish to sell it. Afterward I kept begging him for the picture until eventually he did let me buy it.

Coincidentally, when Gene and I went on a cruise in February 1954, six months after Alice was born, we became friendly with a man named Lipofsky. Years later when I mentioned it to Marvin, he told me that man was his cousin.

I was avidly collecting glass sculptures and placing them throughout our house at first in special glass cabinets I was able to find in large department stores. Later I commissioned Phil Tennant, who taught woodcraft at Herron School of Art, to design custom tables and cabinets for my heavy pieces. These custom designs were then manufactured and installed by Mark Antreasean's design company in Indianapolis.

In the late 1980s Gene was chairman of the building committee and on the board of governors of the Indianapolis Museum of Art. At a meeting one morning in December 1988, each member of this board was asked to contribute a substantial sum toward the addition to the museum under construction at that time. Gene came home and asked me, "What do you think? We could make a sizeable contribution in honor of our anniversary coming up next month." And I said, "Only if the money goes for a glass gallery."

I went down to the museum, and the development director, Mack McKenzie, showed me the spaces that would be available should I place some of my collection there. I did not care for the choices, two rooms on either side of the director's office. Visitors to the museum would either have to know a glass gallery was there or be dependent on a docent's directing them to that space tucked away in a small corner of the third floor. Visitors were most unlikely to see the collection at all in this location.

I wanted this gallery to be in a place where visitors would be attracted by the colorful display immediately to the right of the elevators on the third floor. We had Browning and Day draw plans for what could be done with this space I had chosen. As it turned out, that space had already been promised to a senior curator.

Bob Yassin left the museum shortly thereafter, and Kirk McKinney, who was serving as temporary director, believed this decision should await the arrival of a new director.

I began buying glass to donate to the museum, so the powers-that-be might come to realize how important displaying contemporary studio glass could be for the IMA. Not only would a gallery for contemporary studio glass afford additional interest and pleasure for visitors, but more importantly, our museum might gain national attention for being among the first museums to appreciate the value of this new medium. There was a need to educate the art world about the artistic quality and value of contemporary studio glass, a medium that had not as yet been accepted by many museums and fine art galleries.

Early in February 1989 I told Ferd Hampson, the owner of Habatat Gallery, that I wanted to acquire some important contemporary glass as a gift to the IMA. He told me about a major customer who was having financial difficulties and was preparing to sell his entire collection at auction. Ferd planned to bid for a few of his customers; the auction was coming up the next week at Christie's in New York. I ordered the catalogue and arranged for Ferd to bid on several pieces on my behalf. Two important pieces he secured for me for our museum were a David Hutchhausen *Leitungs Scherbe* and the large Steven DeVries. These were our first gifts to the IMA. Both pieces were on display for a number of years and are currently in storage.

Once the IMA accepted these gifts, I invited Holly Day to our home so I could show her what I had already collected in the past six and a half years. She brought with her Barry Shifman, who came to the IMA from the Getty Museum in California. Barry at that time knew nothing about studio glass art. He was, instead, an expert on Sevre silver who had been hired to be in charge of decorative art at our Indianapolis museum. Barry was fascinated with the glass and called the next day asking if he might come back to see the collection again. He wanted to know more about this medium. I gave him all kinds of literature and information about the glass movement.

In April I took Barry to the glass show in Detroit, where I bought two large pieces at Habatat for our home. Then, later that spring, to further educate him, I sent him to New York for another auction at Christie's. I wanted him to do some bidding there to purchase pieces for me to give to the museum. It was at that time that he was able to secure the Buddha head by Erwin Eisch, a German artist who was a long-time friend of Harvey Littleton. I would not have wanted it in my house but because Eisch was important, I believed it was a desirable piece for the museum to have. There was another piece Barry liked at that auction, and he called during the bidding to ask permission to raise his bid beyond our agreed limit. The bidding was getting high on this Chihuly piece, and since I was cautious about spending money at the time, I let it go. It went to some other museum.

Over a year later I talked to Betsy Rosenfeld, who owned a glass gallery in downtown Chicago, telling her I wanted a six-foot boat by Bertil Vallien. She advised he would be sending her one he was developing in the early fall. Because I was unable to go to her gallery in September, when the piece arrived, I asked if she would hold the boat for me until I would be in Chicago in October for the annual SOFA show. When I arrived at her gallery with Barry to make the purchase, other collectors were waiting for our decision. If I didn't want the piece, they were ready to buy it. I was grateful that collectors and gallery owners were ethical. Reputable dealers would not sell a piece they had promised to hold for a specific customer just to make a quick buck.

When the new IMA director, Bret Waller, came to Indianapolis, we invited him and his wife, Mary Lou Dooley, to stop by the house before dinner to see our collection. Shortly after that meeting, Bret found the best space in the museum for our glass. This spacious room was originally known as the Fesler Gallery, donated by Carolyn Marmon Fesler to be the "Members' Room," overlooking the sculpture garden and White River. The gallery was truly an ideal area full of light and beauty in itself. And so the Eugene and Marilyn Glick Gallery became a reality.

The art museum opened that gallery for contemporary decorative art in 1991. We invited dealers, collectors, and artists to a Saturday dinner at the museum prior to the public opening. Chihuly was on the guest list. He had a commitment in Kansas City that night, but came from Missouri Sunday afternoon. I met him at the museum, and after he saw the gallery, he spent the afternoon at our home. He is—just like an artist. He often wears carpet slippers and casual dress when he goes out, and that is how he appeared with us.

When he was at our home, Chihuly watched the Clarence Thomas hearings on TV and finally came out and looked around. He saw a piece of ceramics he didn't recognize. "Oh, this is a great piece. Who did this?" he asked. And I had to tell him that when Lynda was in junior high, she brought this piece home on the bus the last day of school. It had not come off the wheel as she had planned, and she thought it was awful. She'd hid it in her locker for months, but had to take it home the last day of school that spring before she was sixteen.

He asked for a piece of paper and pencil on which he made a quick sketch of her piece, adding a note that read, "Great piece, Lynda. You should get back to this. Chihuly." To this day it sits by our fireplace, with the note, framed and matted with acid-free paper.

By this time in the mid-nineties, I had collected fifteen or sixteen Joel Philip Myerses, six or seven Chihulys, four Littletons, four Steven Weinbergs, and multiple works of many other noted artists. I was gratified that we were able to donate over two million dollars worth of our glass art to the museum, enabling them to reach the dollars necessary to obtain a large Lilly Foundation matching grant.

There was a lot of investment in these pieces, and Gene never asked about selections or prices, permitting me the freedom to select what I valued. Earlier I had turned down magnificent pieces of jewelry with high price tags because I had no place to wear such valuable pieces and didn't want to spend large amounts of money on jewelry. These works of art, however, enhance our home and the gallery at the Indianapolis Museum of Art. We can enjoy them every day. Since I had never been an extravagant person, it was hard for me to reach a point in life where I was willing to spend that much money. But I came to enjoy these lovely pieces shining with radiant color and ingenious design and picking up and diffusing the sunlight, gracing our rooms and bringing pure enjoyment to our family, friends, and acquaintances.

I extended my glass-collecting interest abroad, participating in one tour with glass collectors sponsored by a gallery in France. It was in Slovakia that I purchased the magnificent blue piece called *Firebird* and added it to the collection during the early nineties.

One of the great joys I've had from collecting glass art is getting to know the artists, collectors, and dealers. I've learned so much from them. Both Chihuly and Littleton have been in our home, as have Myers, DeVries, Weinberg, Stephen Powell, and other well-known artists. Gallery dealers and many collectors have been here as well. To be able to call an artist with questions about his or her work is wonderful. I might ask one of these artists which of his works he believed was his best, and that artist would answer freely.

While much of our collection is still in our home, I like sharing it. I have fun telling visitors stories about experiences I have had along the way with the artists, the galleries, and the people who share my passion for glass. Collecting has added another dimension to my life, and I have grown in the process.

I've especially enjoyed the occasions when I've invited the public to our home to raise money for some of my favorite charities. In 1990 I did a charity show for People of Vision, with thirty-four docents whom I trained for two-hour shifts, assigning each of them to cover a specific area of our home. The glass is literally all over the house. People who bought tickets were assigned certain time segments to see the collection, because I wanted only fifteen people going through the house at any one time. That day People of Vision made $3,400 for the benefit of Prevent Blindness Indiana.

We became friends with one of the major art collecting couples in America, Dorothy (Dodo) and George Saxe. When we scheduled a trip to California, they met us at the airport and took us to their home in Menlo Park, where almost all of their furniture, including accessories, has been crafted by well-known artists. They also have an apartment in San Francisco where they spend weekends. Their glass collection in the Nob Hill area is housed in two adjoining apartments. On one side they live with the glass, as I do, and on the other side they have created a gallery to display their spectacular works of art.

In 2004 the Oakland Museum planned a retrospective of Marvin Lipofsky's work. They asked me for a contribution for the show, and I sent them a check, but I also wanted to see the show. Gene and I went to California, and that gave us an opportunity to be with the Saxes. When we arrived, Dodo told us that Lipofsky had a heart attack and was recovering from bypass surgery. The next day after we viewed the retrospective at the Oakland Museum, Dodo and I bought some flowers for Marvin and went to visit with him at his home.

A number of other artists became good friends as well. This story involves Harvey Littleton. When Bob Payton came to Indianapolis to be head of the philanthropy department of IUPUI, Gene wrote him a letter welcoming him to the city. He invited Bob and his wife to have dinner with us. Later, in the summer, when the Paytons were in France on vacation, they were having dinner in a small village and noticed a couple at the next table speaking English. They struck up a conversation with the couple at that table. When Bob Payton mentioned that he was living in Indianapolis, the gentleman at the other table asked, "Do you know the Glicks?" It was Harvey Littleton with his wife. What a small world it is after all.

There's a whole world of collectors out there, and they share some things in common. I have been privileged to be in the homes of many collectors, and I found that they have followed a path similar to mine. You will see examples of contemporary art on their walls; they too had been collectors of contemporary art before they became interested in glass.

Throughout the 1990s I continued to collect until today there are well over two hundred pieces in the collection. My collection is one of the most extensive in the country, but there are larger ones. The Saxe collection, for instance, is much larger than ours. Irvin Borowsky in Pennsylvania has such a large collection that he has created his own National Liberty Museum, with people from all over the world coming to see his glass. What an asset to the city of Philadelphia! I am no longer looking for more glass. My collection is of a certain period from the days of the flowering of studio glass. And today I deliberately stay away from galleries lest I find more I just may not be able to resist.

Untitled *(from the Contiguous Fragment series), 1988, by Joel Philip Myers.*

David Huchthausen's
Leitungs Scherbe, *ca.*
1987. Purchased for the
Indianapolis Museum of
Art in February, 1989.

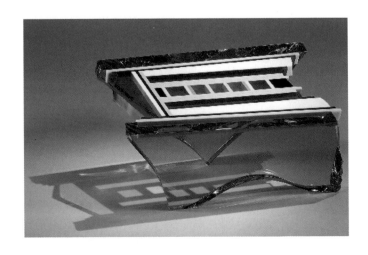

Plate One

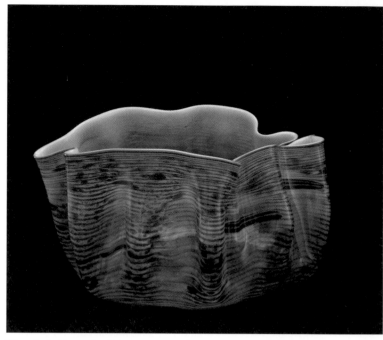

Untitled *(from the "Macchia" series), 1982, by Dale Chihuly. My first Chihuly I bought less than two weeks after I became hooked on glass.*

Athena, *(from the "Mythology Head Vase" series), 1989, by Dan Dailey. One of my favorites. Barely visible green leaves fill the rear of this vase.*

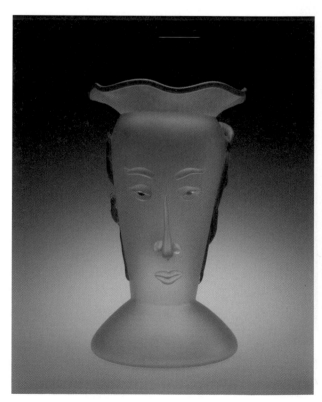

Plate Two

Richard Marquis's (l) Wizard Teapot, *1985. I found in a back room at Habatat Gallery in Boca Raton (r)* Murrine Teapot *1984.*

Marquiscarpa # 23, *1992, by Richard Marquis. One murrini on the top includes the artist's name. Gold leaf finishes the underside of this treasure.*

Plate Three

Marvin Lipofsky's Serie Fratelli Toso — Split Piece, *1977-78. This is my favorite Lipofsky.*

Harvey Littleton's Blue Crown, *(1988), has six major and six minor elements. When I saw a "Crown" in a booklet Harvey sent to me, I wanted one for the IMA. Maureen (his daughter) owns a gallery in Washington, D.C. and made sure I could see this one as soon as it was finished.*

Plate Four

Mark Peiser's Four Seasons Vessel *I placed on a turntable to show visitors how green the trees appear in summer, then clouds and rain are followed by a gold sun as I have turned it full circle. When we spoke to the artist before printing the catalogue for the 1997 IMA show of my glass, the artist told us this is called* The Wheat Piece *from 1978, blown glass with flamework and gold foil.*

Plate Five

Untitled *(fom the "Exotic Bird" series), 1986, by Toots Zynsky. This is one of many consignment pieces a Cincinnati dealer brought to my home for consideration. We became good friends while I was building the collection.*

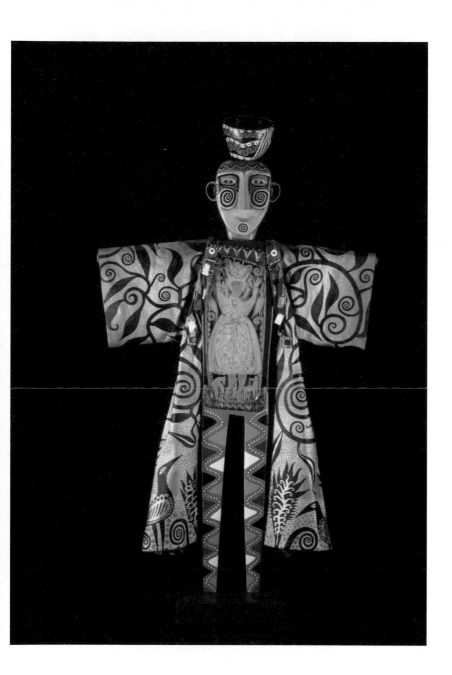

Baudino *(from the "Scarecrow" series), 1992, by Kéké Cribbs. I love this one! This artist is a master of mixed media. She carved and painted the wood doll, painted the canvas robe, and etched and sand–blasted the center glass insert. 40 ½ inches tall. Armspread is 22 ⅞ inches.*

Plate Seven

The Firebird *by Askold Zacko was a spectacular addition to my collection.*

Before the World Was Made *by Richard LaLonda, 1993. At top are phases of the moon, stars, and a bird in the sky. Adam and Eve embrace the world as Eve reaches to temptation (lotus). An animal and the sun are in the middle of ths triptych. Below are two by two in the flood, the evil eye, and the pyramids. All clever and entertaining.*

Plate Eight

Askold Zacko and his wife displayed his magnificent Firebird *when I bought it at his home in Slovakia.*

Our group at the Erwin Eisch gallery in the Black Forest of Germany. Eisch was a long-time friend of Harvey Littleton. To my right is Erwin Eisch. Among those in the photo are: Bob Reiter (next to Eisch); Mimi Reiter and Jan and Jerry Raphael are to my left.

I'm standing in this 1989 photo with Dan Greenberg, a fellow studio glass collector, and Ruth Summers at the Kurland Summers Gallery. We are admiring Richard Jolley's Female Bust with Leaves, *a major piece in the show. I purchased it that night.*

Richard Jolley assisted by his wife (also a glass artist) Tommie Pratt. Female Bust with Leaves, *1989. Glass with cane drawing, sandblasted.*

I'm at home with my collection, photographed by The Indianapolis Star.

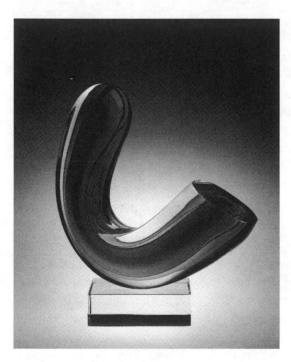

Mobile Yellow Parabolic Arc, *1981, by Harvey Littleton. In 1982 when I discussed this piece with the artist, he referred to it as an inverted "C."*

Finding My Roots

8

$\mathcal{A}$rt wasn't the only interesting thing that absorbed me in the early 1990s. Events were to take me down a road towards finding my birth family roots.

A little background is in order. You will remember that in 1945, when I finally received that affidavit from Michigan asking questions about my birth, what hospital, who was the doctor delivering me and so forth, my mother admitted I was adopted. She cried and told me how she and my dad had taken me home to Detroit after they first saw me in the foster home in New Rochelle, New York.

When I spent a week in Detroit during the next summer, I visited the law office of my legal guardian, Fred Butzel. He had been a friend of the family and I remembered him. He was not in the office at that time, but his office was able to send me a microfilm copy of a document from probate court dated April 4, 1925. It revealed that Abraham and Rose Koffman, after having been confirmed as people of sound moral character and having the ability to support and educate me, were listed as my adoptive parents. The document stated that "the name of said minor child was changed from Minnie Ornstein to Marilyn Ruth Koffman" on that date.

What was important about obtaining this document was that I learned my father's last name was Ornstein, with my name appearing as "Minnie Ornstein." It seemed odd to me in 1945 that anyone would have named me Minnie when I was born. Minnie was a common name of some elderly people in the Koffman family, but no one in my generation had a name like Minnie.

I now suspect there never was a legal birth certificate for this baby born March 8, 1922, with no known living parents, and that "said minor" had no legal name.

My mother had died, and her husband never returned to the hospital. A social worker from a state agency must have been called into the Gouverneur Hospital to remove this nameless and forsaken infant. On the line that asked for the name of the infant in April 1925, I believe "Minnie Ornstein" may have been entered for the convenience of my guardian or officials at an agency in Michigan. It was, in fact, my mother's name, taken from her death certificate. All this I discovered many years later when, through a chain of events, I found my birth family.

By the mid-1940s I was well aware of having been born in New York, and that the Koffmans took me to Detroit from a foster home when I was six months old. I never felt the need to discuss this with any of my friends. I did tell Gene when he proposed to me, but no one else. Interestingly, a boy I dated in the early forties, before my discovery, must have known more than I did, and asked me one day if I was adopted. That thought had never entered my mind. In fact, I told him, "Oh no, relatives often remark about how much I look like my dad." I told him we both had blue eyes, a fair complexion, and curly hair.

This young man must have thought I was a liar. His father was a patient of my uncle, Dr. Lazarus Witt. My uncle probably told my friend's father, his long-time patient and very good friend, about me. Certainly very few in Indianapolis knew about my adoption, and this was the only time before or afterwards that anyone confronted me with such a possibility.

But the admission by my mother in October 1945, and the information on the adoption papers I obtained the next year, left no doubt about my adoption.

It was 1955 before I was able to get a birth certificate from the state of Michigan. For a while I had been satisfied with the document my friend Dorothy had urged me to get over a decade before, because, she said, "everyone should have a birth certificate." It stated I was born in Michigan. This document was legal, but I realized it certainly was not true. As the years passed, the facts surrounding my birth began to bother me, and I grew more curious.

In 1961 I began contacting the Louise Wise Services, through which the Koffmans had worked when they brought me back from New York City to their home in Detroit. I decided to try to find out more about my adoption, but Wise Services was never able to give me any additional information. If I had known my birth father's first name, it might have helped to make the research easier. All I knew for sure was the name Ornstein from that microfilm copy of the adoption paper.

When Gene and I went to New York on business, as Gene was busy at the rent-a-car counter, I would look in the New York City phone book and call Ornsteins to see if I could establish some connection to my father. Of course that phoning was doomed to be unproductive, because it was always a daytime call. If I made any connections at all, I would reach the wife of an Ornstein who would not know anything about what had happened in her husband's family over thirty years earlier.

In June 1961 Gene and I went to Israel on the second Young Leadership Mission trip sponsored by United Jewish Appeal (locally supported by the Jewish Welfare Federation of Greater Indianapolis). I had hoped to visit the Wise adoption agency when we landed in New York on our return from Europe, but it did not work out.

Our family plans were complicated. Gene's dad wanted to take Marianne, then eleven years old, on her first trip overseas. They left Indianapolis ahead of our departure, traveled by ocean liner, and arrived in Paris one day before Gene and I met them when our UJA mission ended. The four of us traveled together throughout France, Germany, and Italy. When we returned to New York, there really was no simple way to visit the adoption agency without spending another night in a hotel. I had been away for the entire month of June; furthermore, I wanted to be home early the next day, July 1, for Arlene's ninth birthday party. Invitations had gone out to her friends before we left for our trip.

I had bought cowboy hats and bandana kerchiefs for all the little girls. They looked so cute on the hayride at Grandview stables, then located on West Sixty-Fourth street.

So we went on home instead of stopping at the adoption agency. After that, as we traveled to New York City, I resumed calling Ornsteins listed in the phone book and even on a few occasions picked up the phone in Miami to see if I might find a relative there. Gene would say to me, "Why do you persist in looking for your father? We have four lovely daughters, a happy home, and a good life. If you found him, he might make life difficult for you."

Gene was right. Life had been so good to us. The birthday party we were planning for Arlene was only one of many family celebrations we enjoyed. All our children had birthday parties, each with a different theme, and there were always games and good food along with ice cream and birthday cake. It was great fun for us as well as for the youngsters. By the time Lynda came along, the older girls pitched in and helped at her parties. I still think of them spinning the little ones around before they attempted to pin a tail on the donkey, and it was always a treat to see the tots scrambling for seats during musical chairs.

Gene was always coming up with surprises for me and the girls. When Arlene was four, he surprised us all by having a pony delivered to our driveway so that the little girls might enjoy pony rides!

The year after we moved into our large home, he had Marianne help him with the guest list, inviting our friends for an after-symphony surprise cocktail party at our house just four evenings before my thirty-ninth birthday. What a thrill! After our twentieth anniversary party we left for our first two-week golfing vacation at Dorado Beach Hotel in Puerto Rico. This became an annual trip each February until 1990, when we found we could spend the entire month of February in our condo in Palm Beach. On our twenty-fifth anniversary we went to Mauna Kea, where Gene enjoyed the *lomi lomi* (Hawaiian massage) each night. We had such a wonderful time I thought this might also be an annual trip each January. But after leaving Hilo at 5 p.m., arriving in Chicago about 6:30 in the morning, and with a change of planes, arriving home in Indianapolis after 9 a.m., it seemed to be such an ordeal that we felt it was just not worth all that effort to return to Mauna Kea.

For birthdays, anniversaries, and Mother's Day, Gene always brings me beautiful surprises. And each and every day he is such a joy. Who could ask for anything more? Certainly "my cup runneth over." The void I had once felt was temporarily sublimated. And I had more than I could have ever imagined in my wildest dreams. So, as Gene advised, in the 1970s, I gave up any hope of finding my roots.

Meanwhile Arlene, inspired by the television show *Roots* in 1977, had begun researching the Biccard family. Adolph Biccard was the grandfather Gene loved so much when he was a child, the grandfather who came home from his office each day with a present for Gene and whose death had devastated him.

As Arlene researched the Biccards, she had the benefit of a Mormon genealogist, Tom Noys. Tom had discovered that Grandpa Adolph had lived in Altdorf, located near Baden-Baden, Germany. So, in 1989 we made another family trip through Europe to visit the Alsace-Lorraine area where Adolph Biccard had lived before coming to America. Gene and I, together with Arlene and her husband Tom, stayed in Brenner's Park Hotel in Baden-Baden and went out to the nearby cemetery at Altdorf, where we saw gravesites of various relatives whose names were on our family tree.

We learned that when Adolph was fourteen, his mother died, and he went to live with family in Gailingen, a small village on the Swiss/German border, until he was seventeen. Then he went to La Havre and took a boat to the USA.

Tom Noys had been to Gailingen the summer before and was able to give us excellent directions to this tiny town; otherwise we would never have found it. We found the cemetery and visited graves of two relatives whose stones both bore the name "Leopold Biccard." The elder Leopold was Gene's great-grandfather and the younger Leopold was a first cousin of Gene's mother. He was a war hero in Germany. A large plaque at the entrance to this cemetery contained a framed certificate presented by the German army: "To Leopold Biccard for service to the Fatherland during World War I." While we were there Gene was able to carry on a good conversation in German with the caretaker of this cemetery, who told him this plaque had originally hung in the synagogue that had been destroyed and was never rebuilt. The plaque was salvaged and was later moved to the cemetery. Our trip was wonderful and enlightening, but Arlene was still not satisfied. She was frustrated that she had not been able to find anything about my birth family.

Shortly after returning from Europe, Arlene found herself sitting next to a social worker at a charity luncheon. This woman worked with Indianapolis families who were adopting children. Arlene discussed our search for clues into my past and told her how much she would like to locate information about my mother. This young woman soon put us in touch with Laurie Thompson, a New York genealogist, who specialized in tracing adoptees' birth family records. Within a two-and-a-half year period, with Laurie working for us, my story gradually unfolded.

It was then that I resumed the search for my birth parents again by contacting the probate court in Michigan to determine if they had further details on my birth through adoption papers I might not have seen. I wrote in March of 1989 and finally in December heard from the Michigan court. Through the documents they sent, I was given the information that my father had disappeared at my birth and that two notices had been placed in New York newspapers in 1923 and 1924 in an attempt to locate him prior to the adoption that had been pending in Michigan. There was no response.

Soon I began to realize the difficulties an adopted child has in locating original records, even if that child is middle-aged or older. The adoption supervisor informed me that the Michigan Probate Court did not have my birth certificate, and even if it did, these records were now sealed by law in Michigan for one hundred years. New York, and most other states, have the same law. It was next to impossible for an adopted child to obtain parents' names or any other information from original records. The supervisor advised me to take my search to New York, the presumed site of my birth, and I determined to pursue this path of inquiry.

By June 21, 1990, Laurie Thompson had sent me copies of several important documents, vital statistics about my original family that were on file in various offices in New York. First I received a copy of my mother's death certificate from Gouverneur Hospital in New York, indicating she died on March 8, 1922. During the birth the placenta had delivered first, and my mother went into shock and died. It appeared from that death certificate that Minnie had lived in New York for nine years and seven months, having come from Russia. She was twenty-four years old when she died.

Laurie would send documents, vital statistics which interested me; then I'd give them to Arlene. In June 1990 I received my parents' marriage license. My father's name was Isidore Ornstein, age twenty-three at the time of the marriage. He had come from Romania and was the son of Orios and Chaya Rosenthal Ornstein. My mother, whose maiden name was Minnie Melman, was shown as the daughter of Joseph and Fannie Lichter Melman, and as the Gouverneur Hospital death record indicated, she had come from Russia. They had surely met in New York and married there. My mother was twenty years old at the time of the marriage on October 17, 1917. The names of my grandparents were listed on the marriage certificate.

And so I confirmed that they were married! I was glad to learn that I was not an illegitimate baby. A full story of my birth continued to emerge from these official documents. When I was born in Gouverneur Hospital and my mother died giving birth, my father never went back to the hospital to claim his baby. He was a young immigrant who undoubtedly felt he could not care for this infant. I believe the baby passed into the hands of the state Department of Public Welfare. Assuming or confirming that the religion of the parents was Jewish, the department turned me over to a Jewish agency. That is how this baby was turned over to Louise Wise's new adoption services agency and was put into a foster home, where the couple who were to be my mother and father found that baby, me.

The Jewish Free Burial Association buried my mother in a Staten Island cemetery in 1922. I requested and received from them a photo of her grave and tombstone, showing her date of death as March 8, 1922, and her age as twenty-four.

Realizing from my contacts with the probate court in Michigan that my father seemed to have disappeared when officials tried to locate him, I surmised he might have jumped into the East River and the body was never found.

But Laurie Thompson dug until she found this was not the case. The research confirmed that Isidore Ornstein had not jumped into the river; he had lived a long life after he left that hospital.

In 1990 I also received a copy of the marriage certificate for Isidore Ornstein and Bessie Roseman, a divorcee. My father had married again in 1924, two years after my mother died in childbirth. At the same time another document arrived. It was a copy of a marriage certificate for Isidore and a Kate Cohen in 1964. My father had re-married after my mother's death not once but twice! And in this same June of 1990 I received a copy of Isidore Ornstein's death certificate dated July 6, 1967. I saw he was listed at the time of his death as a salesman, and that the next of kin was Kate Ornstein.

Also in that early summer of 1990, Laurie sent me my father's intent to apply for naturalization. More information was on this document. Isidore Ornstein had been born in Yassy, Romania, in 1894. He was a very short man, five feet three inches tall, with blue eyes and brown hair, weighing 134 pounds. He had departed Europe from Hamburg heading for America, sailing on the ship *Patricia* in 1907 and arriving in New York City on October 11, 1907. What a coincidence. Rose Budd and Abraham Koffman's marriage had occurred on October 10, 1907, one day before the arrival of my natural father in America. Isidore listed his occupation as "Pharmacist." The application for naturalization was filed in 1917, but he was not accepted for citizenship at that time. He had some studying to do!

I later learned more about Isidore's third wife, Kate Cohen Ornstein.

Her death certificate arrived in August 1990, and it threw more light on my story. On February 5, 1979, Kate died in a nursing home as an old woman of ninety years. Since my father had been dead for over ten years at the passing of Kate, her next of kin was a daughter listed as Lillian Baron.

I expected Lillian Baron would have more information about my father's third wife and my father himself, and I wanted to contact her. First I tried the address listed for Lillian on the death certificate, but that number was no longer valid. Then I tried calling the nursing home to get the daughter's phone number. They told me they did not have her phone number.

I gave the nursing home my phone number and requested that if they were ever in contact with her, I would like to have her call me. Five minutes later, my phone rang. It was the woman from the nursing home. She had just talked to Lillian Baron, who was willing to speak to me. So they did have her number after all. I talked to Lillian, who was now living in Sunrise, just west of Ft. Lauderdale, Florida. When I told her who I was, she said, "Oh, I met you. Don't you remember me? I was at your home with my husband, my mother, and your father. You were playing ball in front of your home with your son. He was about to have a Bar Mitzvah." What was this? Lillian was mistaking me for someone who had a son, whom she believed was Isidore's daughter.

It seemed reasonable that this woman whom Lillian Baron had once visited years before must have been a half-sister or stepsister of mine. My father and Bessie could have had a child together, so there could be a half-sister. Or it could be a stepsister if Bessie had a child before she married my father. Bessie was listed as divorced on the marriage license. Lillian did not know any details beyond what she was telling me in this phone conversation.

Lillian Baron had left New York just six months before we talked. If I had located her sooner, she would have had many pictures to send me, but she had discarded almost all of the family photos when she and her husband David moved to Florida. I told her that Gene and I would be in Florida in the winter and I would like to meet them. They came up to our apartment in Palm Beach that November and we had dinner and a good talk.

Lillian and David brought a home movie of my father dancing with Lillian's mother at their wedding. They told me a lot I did not know. They had just loved "Izzie" Ornstein, finding him fun to be around. Izzie was a shoe salesman, a member of the shoeman's union, but he did not always get to the shoe store on time or with great regularity. He did not like to work all the time, seemingly satisfied living on a very limited income.

Kate had been married two times before, just as Isidore had. He and Kate Cohen were together less than four years before this biological father of mine had a prostate operation and died three weeks later, at the age of seventy-three. Perhaps he had an embolism or stroke. From his pictures it is evident that my father was, as the record had stated, short and stocky, and I suspect my mother must have been taller. But we have no way of knowing.

In 1991 I received Isidore's final naturalization papers from Laurie. The papers showed that my father had learned to speak English and had been sworn in as an American citizen finally in February 1920.

These naturalization papers contained more revelations. When I was born, Isidore Ornstein had a three-year-old child! The Louise Wise agency had told me there were no children surviving when Minnie Ornstein died, and I had accepted that statement. They truly never had this information. The name "Frances" was on Isidore's naturalization papers. She had been born on February 28, 1919. The sister I'd imagined to be a half or stepsister, whom Lillian had seen years ago, was my own blood sister, sharing the same mother and father I had at birth. Frances was the sister I'd yearned for as long as I could remember. This revelation was a vital key to finding my family. But there was a lot more I needed to know.

In 1922 Isidore had evidently decided he could not take care of either three-year-old Frances or the new infant. I later found out he had sent Frances to live with relatives in Boston, but we still do not know whether she was living with my mother's relatives or Isidore's family.

Two years after my mother died, Isidore married Bessie. Bessie never learned to speak English, but they continued to live in the Coney Island Jewish community, where in those days all the shopkeepers and most of the people spoke Yiddish. They could live very comfortably in their Coney Island neighborhood with no need to speak the English language.

When Bessie married Isidore, she insisted that he bring his daughter back to Coney Island, where Bessie loved and cared for her. Frances had been with relatives for two years at that time.

But how did I learn these details about Bessie and my father? Some had come out from my talks with the daughter of Isidore's third wife. But

Lillian and her husband could not even remember the name of the young woman whom they had seen playing ball with her son "on the Island." Now, after the arrival of the naturalization papers, I saw that the name of my sister was "Frances." So now I had a vital clue to pursue. I realized I would have to find my sister, but that might be impossible since I knew only her first name. How desperately I wanted to find her. But how would I do that? Where would she be today? I found out details of this sister's life in a most unusual way.

What a shame Lillian Baron did not know my sister's married name. That bothered me terribly for over a year. How would we ever find her? I thought I might put a notice in the Jewish newspapers in New York City and the *National Jewish Post* headquartered in Indianapolis. I even considered writing a little article entitled "Looking for Frances," hoping to have it published in the *Reader's Digest*. It was like looking for the proverbial needle in a haystack.

My only hope was that perhaps a marriage license would surface. Then, in mid-March 1992, when I returned from a few weeks in Florida, I found the most exciting mail from Laurie Thompson. It was just what I had been hoping to find, the marriage license of Frances Ornstein and Edmund S. Ellison.

I was looking for a real human being now, and here was the name I needed. How very fortunate it was that my sister married a man with an unusual name! Had she married a Sam Cohen or Marvin Levy, I would have reached a dead end after coming so close to finding the family I had been seeking for so long. This document was the key that would open the door to all the revelations that followed.

But the trail in New York had grown cold by the time Laurie Thompson sent me the marriage license. She informed me there was no Edmund Ellison with a driver's license in the state of New York. I could not trace him that way. Gene, however, reminded me that it was common for people from New York to retire to Florida. Perhaps Edmund and Frances were now in Florida. So I decided to try searching in Florida for my missing sister. Today it would be impossible to do what I did in 1992. I called the information operator in area code 305 and asked her to check Miami, Hollywood, and Ft. Lauderdale for the listing of Edmund Ellison. Then I asked for further assistance.

There were two Edmund Ellisons in Miami and one in Ft. Lauderdale. One Miami Ellison had an unlisted phone. I began with that one.

"Would you please call Mr. Ellison and ask him to call me?" I pleaded with the operator.

"What is the nature of your emergency?" she asked.

I told her my story. "I'm not supposed to do this but I will call for you." She got back to me and said, "That is not your relative." I tried the other Miami Ellison. He was not the Ellison I was seeking, either.

I attempted contacting the one in Ft. Lauderdale, but I got no answer. I simply couldn't reach him in the evenings when I tried to call. Several days later, having forgotten to go to my morning tennis class (I never was very good at it), I reached the number in Ft. Lauderdale. It was just about noon on a Friday. "Is this Edmund Ellison?" I asked when a man's voice answered. "Yes." I got right to the point. "Is your wife Frances?" He replied, "Frances is dead and I just lost my second wife."

He had been married to his second wife for twenty years, but had lost her on Christmas Day. This was mid-March. He was still grieving.

Still, he was willing to meet me a month later in Florida. He came with a lady friend, so his grief seems to have been eased by that time. When I first called him in March, he was a little bit suspicious of me, not knowing what I wanted. Less than a year earlier he had talked to someone who was selling family crests and Edmund wanted to be careful now. But he suggested I might talk to his daughter, Barbara, in Long Island, New York. He gave me her phone number and advised me to wait until evening to call her. He also told me her husband, Joel, was a brother to the comedian Billy Crystal. And Joel Crystal was every bit as funny as Billy!

This daughter, Barbara Crystal, was teaching English at Long Beach High, where her husband was an art teacher. When I talked to her at her home in the evening she was absolutely amazed and thrilled to know she had an Aunt Marilyn and Uncle Eugene and cousins. You can only imagine the emotions this call had stirred up for my niece and me. We talked for a long time. When Arlene and Marianne talked to her a little later, Barbara told them she had cried for forty-five minutes after first talking to me.

She told me the story of her mother, my sister Frances. Then, her brother, Alan, later added more details. Frances told her children that during her childhood in the Depression, she had experienced poverty. She urged Barbara and Alan to eat all the food on their plates because at times there had been so little on hers. Frances had been a good student. When she attended high school with excellent grades, she was offered a full scholarship to a private educational institution, the Ethical Culture School. But Isidore and Bessie did not allow her to accept. She struggled with them for much of her high school years because they wanted her to drop out of school and go to work. They did not see the value of education. Bessie was illiterate. After graduation Frances went to work as a seamstress in the garment district. Later she was employed by a milliner.

Frances resented Isidore because he did not allow her to accept the scholarship and because he had sent her to Boston when her mother died giving birth to a baby girl. Frances always wanted to know more about her mother and this sister, who might have survived. But Isidore refused to talk about it.

As the stories emerged from Barbara and Alan, I began to form a more complete image of my father. The Barons had told me he was charming, that they loved this man with such a pleasing personality, that he liked to dance and to play cards. But he never had any money, and they would often give him a few dollars so he could take their mother to the movies. He was totally irresponsible. One reason the records were so sparse on Isidore Ornstein was that he did not own a home nor even pay his rent regularly. He would simply leave the places he occupied when he was about to be evicted.

Later Alan told me this was a pattern he observed throughout his childhood. When Frances took him as a boy to visit Bessie and Isidore, they seemed to be in a different apartment every visit. Barbara explained a major reason for her mother's resentment towards her father was his irresponsibility. Frances often told her of instances when he claimed to be looking for a job but went to the movies instead. Bessie was the source of strength in his family, as our mother must have been before she died. I came to believe both my sister and I inherited a lot of our mother's genes. From what I have learned from her family and friends, Frances and I were very much alike in personality as well as appearance. By thinking about both of her daughters, I surmise my mother was an energetic and lively young woman.

When she was twenty-two, Frances married a very pleasant and hard-working man, Edmund Ellison, whom Gene and I had met in Florida. Ed Ellison and his partner had owned a button-jobbing business in the garment district of New York, taking button orders from garment manufacturers and placing them with button-makers. One day while they were lunching at the automat, Ed's business partner introduced him to

Frances. It was love at first sight. Later Eddie became sole owner of this business with offices located across from Macy's Department Store.

After they were married, Frances and Ed had a Cape Cod home in Mt. Kisco (Westchester County). Barbara had been born in 1942 and her sister Karen was born six years later. They were happy in the Mt. Kisco home until three-month-old Karen died of sudden infant death syndrome while napping in her carriage on the front porch. This was a terrific shock for the Ellisons. Although Barbara was only six years old at the time, she told me, "I will never forget my mother's wails of anguish as she held the dead baby in her arms—it was a horror." After this tragedy it was too painful for Frances to live in that house. They sold it and moved to Long Beach, near the ocean and the boardwalk. This beach-side neighborhood reminded her of the best of her childhood in Coney Island.

My sister was active in a variety of causes, from Hadassah to PTA and local politics. Like me she enjoyed art and visited museums. Temple Emanuel in Long Beach was very important to her, and she also loved to travel. She dearly loved her husband and appreciated the life she had with him. Frances was described as a feisty woman, sometimes strong-willed and dominant, but Barbara and Alan report she was also exceptionally loving and valued her children above all else. After the move to Long Beach, Frances had another baby who lived only one day. She must have been overjoyed when her son Alan arrived twelve and a half years after Barbara was born.

Frances and Bessie remained very close. Barbara recalled one day riding with her mother as they took chicken soup to Bessie. Barbara told me she hated to go to Coney Island and was complaining about these weekly visits, when her mother admitted, "I love Bessie dearly, but she isn't my real mother. And I think I have a sister somewhere. I suppose there is no way I could find her." My sister had been told her own mother had died when Frances was three. But Bessie raised her from the time she was five years old, and she really knew no other mother. As Alan grew older, after Barbara left for college, Frances often spoke of a sister whom she would never be able to find.

My niece told me about her mother's illness. Frances had an ugly melanoma on her ankle and thought she was cured after it had been removed and she had undergone chemotherapy. But seven and a half years later, it metastasized and she developed a malignant brain tumor. After suffering for many months, she died in 1972 at age fifty-four. Alan was seventeen and in his senior year at Long Beach High School when his college acceptance arrived. Recently he wrote to me, "I believe that given the importance she placed on education, she was able to extend her life through inner will until she received this important news. She battled and battled to live until that day. I remember when I told her about my acceptance, in her weakened state she took my hand and squeezed it, giving me a hug from her hospital bed."

In college Barbara majored in English and minored in dance. She received both her undergraduate and master's degrees at the University of Michigan.

Alan earned his bachelor of arts degree from the University of Michigan, where he was Phi Beta Kappa. Then, with a full scholarship from the University of Pennsylvania, he did his graduate work at Wharton School of Business.

When I talked to Barbara that first time in March, we decided to meet as soon as possible. Our meeting was set for April 1992. Arlene and Marianne flew to New York with Gene and me, while Alice flew up from Boca to meet us there. Gene was thrilled and enthusiastic. He wanted to rent a helicopter from the Kennedy airport but that wasn't feasible. There wasn't any place for a helicopter to land near the Crystal home in Long Island.

As we arrived, Barbara, Joel, and Alan with his son David, then close to two years old, were there to greet us. Barbara was particularly moved because she said she could have picked me out anywhere—I looked so much like her mother. They all agreed on that. We drove over to the Holiday Inn near the airport for lunch.

From there the Crystals took us to their home, where we spent the afternoon looking through their photo albums until it was time to enjoy our first family dinner, the second night Seder together. It was a poignant moment for me, considering that in Detroit on the night of the second Seder in April of 1933, my father, A. J. Koffman, the only father I ever knew, died in Shaarey Zedeck synagogue. What a coincidence it was, fifty-nine years later on the Jewish calendar, in New York on the night of the second Seder in April of 1992, I was united with my birth family, descended from the mother and father I was never to know. The fact that it was the same date on the Jewish calendar strikes me as being miraculous. There have been so many strange coincidences and so many surprises in my life that I sometimes wonder if I was truly destined to live this storybook tale.

Alan was an economist with a bank in Buffalo, New York, when we first met. He seemed rather reserved and very bright. Alan and Lorna's daughter, Katherine Frances (Kate), was born three years after we met the family.

Before the Seder dinner, as Barbara brought out her pictures, I saw a photo which is probably of my mother. The woman in the picture was standing with someone who appears to be her relative, perhaps a brother.

After our delicious holiday dinner, Gene and Marianne flew back to Indianapolis, but Arlene, Alice, and I spent the night in Joel's mother's home around the corner from Barbara and Joel's house. Some years later when we went to New York to see Billy Crystal's one-man show *700 Sundays*, we realized the backdrop on that stage was a replica of the front of the Crystal home where I slept with Arlene and Alice in April 1992.

Joel's mother was spending the winter in her apartment on Collins Avenue in Miami Beach. On my next trip to Florida, I was able to visit her there. After securing a driver for the day, I went to Eddie Ellison's home in Plantation, a suburb of Ft. Lauderdale. Eddie brought out pictures and letters and newspapers, mostly about Alan, of whom he was so very proud. Then we took Eddie with us and drove to Collins Avenue, where we visited Helen Crystal Greenfield and her second husband, Al, at their apartment on the beach. We all had lunch together in the restaurant right in that apartment building.

After lunch my driver took us to see the Holocaust Museum in Miami before taking Eddie back to his home. It was such a joy to be with this extended family, all of whom could not get over how much I resembled my sister not only in appearance but especially in personality.

We got to know so many of these interesting people in my sister's extended family. We came to know Joel's Uncle Bern, brother of Joel's father Jack, who died when Billy was fifteen. A few years ago Billy Crystal's daughter, Lindsay, made a documentary featuring Uncle Bern, which aired on television. Barbara gave me a copy of this video.

Early one Saturday in July of that year, 1992, Tom and Arlene accompanied me to New York. While they were at a baseball game, I rented a car and driver for three hours. I decided to have lunch with Uncle Bern, who is quite an interesting character. He showed me his art gallery, which was in no way contemporary—but I certainly appreciated seeing the antiques he collected and getting to know Uncle Bern and his sweet wife, Debra. They are a dear couple. After leaving them, I went to Soho to visit the Guggenheim Museum and on to some of the art galleries, where I bought a few small glass sculptures at Heller Gallery that day.

I had made an appointment to meet Laurie Thompson for a drink in a coffee shop before dressing for the theater. I wanted to tell her about my family and thank her for all her help. And I wanted her to help me locate my mother. Because Laurie was convinced that my mother must have immigrated from Russia through Canada, she went on to explain that there would be no record of Minnie Melman at Ellis Island. It would be difficult, she told me, to find the details of that immigration. Laurie was never able to give us any further information.

Gene flew into New York later in the day and met us that evening at the theater, where Barbara and Joel as well as Alan and his wife, Lorna, were our guests at a Broadway musical. After the show we all walked to the Russian Tea Room for a late-night supper.

In April 1992 I had begun correspondence with the cemetery where my mother was buried. Since my father had provided a monument for the grave several years after her death, I arranged perpetual care for the gravesite and a footstone for the grave that reads, "Minnie Ornstein, mother of Marilyn Glick and Frances Ellison." I now wanted to have some sort of closure with the grave of my mother and Barbara's grandmother. So, on the morning after we enjoyed the theatre and dinner with this family, we all assembled at the cemetery in Staten Island.

I had located a rabbi to conduct a brief ceremony and had worked out a prayer based on some traditional ones Rabbis Sandy and Dennis Sasso, of Beth-El Zedeck congregation in Indianapolis, had sent to me. And so at the unveiling of the stone marker, the rabbi read this prayer that expressed the sentiments of all of us, but particularly Barbara and me:

Eternal God, standing by the grave of our blessed mother and grandmother, Minnie Melman Ornstein, we regret that we were not privileged to know her and to love her. But we are grateful for the gift of life she gave her daughters, Frances and Marilyn. We thank God for making her a woman of courage and a woman of substance. For as we identify ourselves with her life, her hopes, and her traditions, the traditions of an eternal people, we ourselves take on the aspect of eternity. May we so live that when our years draw to a close we will be remembered for good and for blessing. Oh God, strengthen us so that we may bear the loss of both Minnie and Frances. May we do so without despair, but rather may we devote our actions and our aspirations to honor our departed. With love we consecrate this marker to the memory of a woman of valor, Minnie Melman Ornstein.

"May her soul be bound in the bond of life."

Since the time I found Frances's family, we have shared numerous happy celebrations. The Crystals and the Ellisons were in Indianapolis for Brian's Bar Mitzvah and for Jackie's wedding and our huge fiftieth anniversary party at the IMA. Gene and I and all of our daughters plus Jackie went to New York when Barbara and Joel's daughter Faithe married Paul Ferrante. Faithe and Jackie are the same age and became good friends when we were all together in Florida for Christmas 1992.

Later, in 2005 all the family traveled directly from the Greenbrier to Long Beach to attend Jonathan Crystal's wedding, I spoke with Uncle Bern again. I loved the cute drawings he had created to be enjoyed by the wedding guests as they waited for the bridal party to come down the aisle. I said to him, "Uncle Bern, if I send you photos of my great-grandchildren, would you do some of these drawings for them?"

"I don't have time to do that, I'm sorry," he answered. Uncle Bern was ninety-one and in a wheelchair, but he was so busy he didn't have time for all the activities he'd have liked to do. He told me he was getting ready for a show, and he needed to create more of his own drawings for the show. He was also designing greeting cards for Target.

We have invited Barbara and Alan's families to join us from time to time as our guests at the Greenbrier Hotel in West Virginia. Once, while my niece and her husband spent a week at our condo in Florida, Joel's mother was able to come up to be with us for a Valentine's dinner and dancing at the club. When Helen was dancing with Gene, she said to him, "I'm glad I have only three sons because Joel is a head taller than Rip, who is a head taller than Billy. If I had had any more boys, they would have been midgets." Humor must run in that family.

In writing this story for my children, grandchildren, great-grandchildren and all the generations to follow, I have come to realize what a miraculous chain of events made all of this possible. I would never have known I had been adopted if my friend Dorothy had not urged me to get my birth certificate. If I had not made that search, I would never have known the Koffmans were not my birth parents, and would never have come upon my birth father's first name. Then, if my daughter, Arlene, had not been so persistent and intent on tracing my "roots," I would not have found Laurie Thompson, who was willing and able to research the family documents in a way I never could have. And if my sister had not married a man named Edmund Ellison, I might never have found out who she was and discovered this most special family.

If these things had not occurred in the way they did, I would still feel in some strange way incomplete, not quite real. I still cannot put my feelings into words, but once I found this family the void was gone, and I am so much more confident and wholly at peace with myself and all of my precious family.

It always amazes me how very closely I resemble my sister, Frances, and how much her daughter looks like me. If you line up our four girls in a row and add Barbara, then ask a stranger which one of these young women is Marilyn's daughter, that stranger would select Barbara! I can understand the physical similarity, but the fact that my personality mirrors that of my sister I never will understand.

It is always a difficult emotional experience for Barbara when we are together, because she feels such mixed emotions of joy and sadness all at the same time. I am so much like her mother that her eyes fill with tears. While she is happy to have me with her, it is almost as if her mother is now alive again. The closeness they shared while Frances lived and the suffering they experienced during her illness stir up a longing for her mother, who died too soon. Barbara and I have a wonderful, unusual relationship for which we are grateful.

Some years later, watching television one day, I noted a report on the deplorable condition of some cemeteries in the New York City area, and the Staten Island cemetery (Mt. Richmond, formerly Ocean View) was one of them. Graves were neglected and grass was overgrown in the cemetery where my mother lies buried. Seeing that, I was glad we had paid our reverence to that lonely grave, and that now it was being cared for.

May her soul truly be bound in the bond of life.

Then, and ever afterwards, I have been thinking of all the other adoptees who may have had difficulties similar to what I've experienced searching for my birth parents. I have never resolved in my own mind the problem that the laws of the land present.

I think my feelings are best expressed in a letter I had sent to the Louise Wise Services at the time I was desperately searching for information about my birth and parents in 1990. Here it is, reflecting the frustration I felt during the period before I found my sister and her family.

I am now 68 years old. My daughter and I have been attempting to get more information about my background and have been in touch with you in the past. You were unable to give any identifying information at those times. However, with what I have now learned I see no reason why you cannot give me a copy of all the records you have in your files.

Through a genealogist in your area I have been able to acquire the death certificate of my natural mother, Minnie Ornstein, who did in fact die in childbirth at the Gouverneur Hospital in Brooklyn. She was buried by the Hebrew Free Burial Association. I have additional information on these various marriage licenses and death certificates. How unfortunate that you were not able to release any further information to me earlier while [my father] was still alive. I began searching for him in 1961 when it would have been possible to meet the man. I cannot help but wonder if he and Bessie had any children together. I want nothing from this family but kinship. I was the only child of Rose and Abraham Koffman. I longed for a sister. I don't need anything from such a relationship and laws about invasion of privacy make no sense to me at this late date. . . . There may be a younger half brother or sister. I would like to know them and know about their life. I would like to obtain some photographs to show my children and grandchildren and note whether there might or might not be family resemblances. If available, I would just love to have a picture of my real mother, Minnie. Just any family photos would be so interesting. It just seems to me that since Isidore Ornstein lived in Brooklyn from the time of his marriage to my mother until he died that if sufficient effort had been made, he could have been found. I could have helped him.

For the way I feel about this matter, there will never be closure.

Isidore Ornstein at his Bar Mitzvah.

Above, from my niece's album, is my birth mother, Minnie Ornstein. On the right you see Minnie and a man I suspect was her brother.

Frances as a child living with her father Isidore and his second wife Bessie.

Bessie, Frances, and Isidore. My sister was fourteen at the time.

The wedding day of Frances and Edmund Ellison.

Barbara with Grandma Bessie and Grandpa Isidore.

My sister Frances (seated) celebrates Passover with Bessie and Isidore.

Barbara kisses her mother, my sister Frances, goodbye as she heads off to Girl Scout camp.

Here is Frances at Barbara's wedding reception dancing with the groom, Joel Crystal.

Alan Ellison and his two children, David (born July 11, 1990) and Katherine (born June 18, 1995).

Our great-grandson Joel Barrett is crying in Jackie's arms while an amused Billy Crystal wonders if he is causing it. We were all at Barbara's home for the informal pre-nuptial dinner, when Faithe married Paul Ferrante.

Gene B. Glick

COMPANY, INC.

8330 Woodfield Crossing Boulevard
P.O. BOX 40177   (317) 253-3606
Indianapolis, Indiana 46240

Gene B. Glick
President

March 30, 1992

Dear Barbara & Alan:

This is not going to be a long letter - it is much more
satisfying to have lengthy communication by phone - but
we simply must try to convey our joy at having found you,
given such long odds that it would happen. Even the simple
words of family relationships, Niece and Nephew, take on
special meaning for us as we were both brought up in single-
child families, and so you are the first relatives we can
address this way. And it is such deep pleasure to be able
to do so!

You may remember through the phone conversation that this
happy result is the culmination of a search which began in
1961. Unsuccessful at that time, the investigation lang-
uished for years until our daughter, Arlene, supplied her
own brand of dedication and persistence to the matter. It
was her creative and ingenious interest in our family's
genealogy, on both sides, that resulted in this discovery
of family we knew nothing about. She is elated, of course,
as are we.

But the word "elated" is too mild for our feelings; as a
matter of fact, our emotions are truly too deep for ordi-
nary words, as you no doubt appreciate. We can only hope
you share our joy in this discovery and if you do you have
some idea of what we feel.

We're looking forward with tremendous anticipation to meeting all of you, now that this search "Looking for Frances"
has come to such an exhilarating conclusion. It is heart-
warming to know there are other individuals in this nation
of millions of souls who share a common heritage; relatives
of whom we knew nothing a few short days ago. We await with
delight our first "family reunion".

With love,

Marilyn & Gene

Gene B. Glick
President

Gene B. Glick

COMPANY, INC.

8330 Woodfield Crossing Boulevard
P.O. BOX 40177   (317) 253-3606
Indianapolis, Indiana 46240

March 30, 1992

Hi Arly:

There is no way we can express our admiration and appreciation to you for your loving dedication and persistence
which led to the discovery of long-lost relatives, except
to say those words in the context of the love we feel for
you.

It was your creative ingenuity which brought it about, and
we acknowledge the debt which cannot be repaid, except as
you yourself know what it means to all of us to have discovered "family". Because of your interest in our heritage
and determination to seek it out, we have discovered relatives which would otherwise have remained forever hidden.

The joy which your resolution and tenacity has brought to
all of us is impossible to measure; it will bubble forth
over the years as the relationships blossom and grow.

You were the indomitable captain who led the voyage of discovery and found the passage leading to the revelation
which is so amazing and satisfying. Your leadership was
the impetus which finally reached the goal which means so
much to all of us.

Thank you, Lil' Arly, thank you. Those words would be inadequate, except you know they come from the depths of our
hearts.

Love & Kisses,

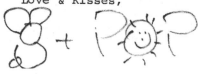

We are at our temple for Brian Grande's Bar Mitzvah in December 1992. Lorna and Alan Ellison, Rose Rossman, (Eddie's lady friend) Eddie Ellison, Marilyn and Gene, Barbara and Joel Crystal.

Marianne and Mike Woods, Karyn, Alice and Andrew Meshbane, Barbara and Joel Crystal, Allison (behind fan), Dora Meshbane, Lauren Schwartz at the Greenbrier in 2004..

My niece Barbara and I are very close.

Barbara at Greenbrier.

In July of 2005 our family went directly from the Greenbrier to attend the wedding of Jonathan and Vanessa in Long Beach, New York.

All our daughters, their husbands, and the Barretts went to celebrate the wedding of our grand-niece, Faithe, to Paul Ferrante. Here is a recent photo of the Ferrante family (l-r) baby Shane, Dad, Holly, Mom and Laura (their middle child).

The Art of Giving

9

As the 1990s unfolded and a new century began, many activities placed us squarely in the heart of our community. Perhaps the major philanthropic effort of my life has been prevention of blindness. Let me tell you how I came to be involved.

It began in the 1960s, when I attended a membership tea for North Group of the Women's Committee of the Indianapolis Symphony Orchestra. A friend of mine, Flo Greenberg, then president of North Group, asked me to be chairman of a committee soliciting advertising for the symphony season program book. Since Gene and I have never taken out ads in publications like this, I declined that chairmanship but said, "I'll be happy to help you with membership, if you want me to serve on your board."

A lovely lady, Dr. Lavonne Washington, a dentist in Indianapolis, was already in charge of collecting dues for membership, so I worked with her for several years until our terms expired. She called me subsequently and asked if I would come on the board of Young Audiences. This group sponsors programs with musicians from our symphony orchestra. The musicians hired by Young Audiences entertain schoolchildren throughout Indiana while they familiarize these young people with their respective instruments and help them to develop an appreciation for classical music. I agreed to work with this group.

As I served on that board, I found they needed more financial support, so I developed a fund-raising campaign. To raise funds, I had phone-a-thons at the Glick Company office, and we sent out bulk mailings directly from my home.

Lavonne Washington called again a number of years after my active involvement with Young Audiences. She told me her husband was president of the Indiana chapter of Prevent Blindness America and invited me to come onto their board. I had never even heard of this organization.

"Lavonne," I said. "I don't want to be on any more boards at this time. But I would be willing to meet with the board and possibly be able to offer some advice." After my first meeting with the board, I could see they were in need of much more community recognition of the services they render to so many people throughout the Hoosier State. I recommended they form an auxiliary. So, for another time in my life, I ended up in charge of the very job I had suggested needed to be done.

In 1979 I invited Irma Sauer, Ceil Schnelker, and Florence Maxwell, who had previously founded vital auxiliaries, to be my guests for lunch. These ladies were about twenty years my senior. Sue Hetherington, then executive director of the Indiana Society to Prevent Blindness, joined us that day. Because this worthwhile organization was to celebrate its thirtieth anniversary in March 1980, that year seemed to be the perfect time to launch our auxiliary.

I took out my 3x5 cards and got to work. During this time Gene was occupied at night with business planning meetings. He would be at the office until two or three o'clock in the morning, and I would sometimes be up all night developing this file.

With a file of five thousand 3x5 cards, we began raising funds. I had already asked forty community leaders to become "founders" in this endeavor. In the fall of 1979 we began having planning meetings in my home. Then, when Mayflower moving company donated the printing for five thousand three-in-one postcard promotional pieces we were ready. I arranged for mailing parties at my home, using eight foot tables set up in the recreation room downstairs. The founders were invited for whatever time they had free from 9:30 a.m. to 5 p.m. to work on this mailing. In just two days, we had hand-addressed all of the promotional pieces. Shoe boxes with zip codes marked on them helped us sort for the bulk mailing. It was the same system I'd used for the Borinstein Guild and Young Audiences.

It is interesting to note that at that time auxiliaries of not-for-profit 501(c)(3) organizations were able to send pre-sorted bulk mail for just five cents each piece. Today the price has increased substantially for this type of mailing. Now, most auxiliaries are required to use first class postage for all their mailing.

We'd break at noon for lunch of Chinese food or another easy spread set up by our cook Edith Shelton. Our dining table accommodates sixteen and it was always fun, with lots of camaraderie. After lunch, we'd continue the work of addressing, stuffing, sealing, and sorting this huge stack of mail.

During this time we were meeting regularly at my home planning a benefit to increase awareness of the parent organization then known as the Indiana Society to Prevent Blindness. We decided to have a Sunday brunch to be held on March 15, 1980. Our guest speaker was the executive head of our national organization, then located in New York. The Tom Mullinix jazz band provided music. L. Strauss and Company, a fine retail store located on the southeast corner of Washington and Illinois streets, provided outfits for an elegant fashion show of men and women's clothing. All of our forty founders brought their friends and families, purchasing tables for groups of ten at the Sheraton by the airport, now called Adams Mark. Mayflower donated the printing for our invitations and programs.

Committees handled all that was needed for a successful affair. The fashion show committee, headed by Jo Fleener, selected the models, and the models' families all came, of course. Thaddeus Larson, whose wife was one of our founders, was managing director of L. Strauss and Company, so that is how Strauss was induced to provide the fashion show for us. My neighbor, Vera Lamprecht, whose husband was the chief executive at Boehringer Mannheim Company, was also on my committee. The Lamprechts were friendly with the head of Elizabeth Arden and asked him to donate the favors. At that time the Eli Lilly Company owned Elizabeth Arden, and the elegant gifts they donated for the guests were large and attractive nylon tote bags filled with useful cosmetics. We made $15,000 on that first luncheon.

We kept track of everyone who had contributed at least five dollars. Now that these donors were familiar with Prevent Blindness, we had a prospect list for our first drive for membership in the auxiliary. When proposals were offered for naming our auxiliary, the founders all voted in favor of my suggestion, "People of Vision." Our deadline for charter membership was September 30, 1980. As of this writing, our roster includes 591 members. Not all of these people are active members, but their membership dues each year are shared with Prevent Blindness Indiana and add up to a sizeable contribution.

In March 1950 the Indiana Society to Prevent Blindness became the first affiliate of this national organization. Today the name is Prevent Blindness Indiana and we are one of the strongest affiliates of Prevent Blindness America.

A portion of what Prevent Blindness Indiana receives is sent to Prevent Blindness America. The national office provides us with promotional pieces and educational mailings. In this way we are able to offer valuable information and important suggestions for prevention of blindness to donors and members of POV. The national organization invests in research and provides guidance to its affiliates. Just as we help to support them, they give support to PBI.

In recent years People of Vision has been working with Prevent Blindness Indiana on a major fundraiser we call the Eye Ball. Our current president is Margaret Bannister Krauss, a bright, well-organized, and conscientious volunteer. Under her leadership, in 2006 we included an internet auction as part of the fund-raising. Net profit from the 2006 Eye Ball was $50,000.

There is so much information people need to know. Unfortunately many people do not realize how important it is to have annual visits with an eye specialist, who will dilate both eyes to check for problems. If glaucoma is caught early enough, it can be treated successfully. Since half of all blindness can be prevented, all eye diseases should be treated as early as possible. Staff and volunteers from Prevent Blindness Indiana travel throughout the state to test adults for glaucoma. Workers in factories need eye protection, and educational programs for these workers are provided by Prevent Blindness America as well.

Children in particular should be checked and their eye problems addressed before it is too late to remediate eye problems. For example amblyopia, a problem in which one eye wanders, must be corrected when a child is young, or the sight in the child's "lazy eye" may be lost completely. Teams of People of Vision volunteers go to Indianapolis schools to test children for a variety of eye problems and to encourage children to wear helmets while they play sports and ride their bicycles.

In February, 2008, a group of volunteers will be going to Washington, D.C. to lobby for a law requiring a mandatory check of each infant's eyes by an opthalmologist before the baby leaves the hospital. The problem is that most pediatricians are not aware of a genetic cancer usually undetected until it is too late to prevent blindness and even early death of the affected babies. Currently hearing tests are mandatory for new babies.

Sadly, to date no appropriate eye tests are required.

There was no personal or family eye problem that led me to become involved in this cause at the time I founded People of Vision. Ironically, it was some years later when Gene discovered that he had developed glaucoma. It was years before the pressure build-up in his eyes showed up on the tests during his annual physical exams.

People of Vision has continued to occupy much of my time. Its success over the past quarter century has given me considerable satisfaction. POV was my baby, and in looking over my life of community service, I realize I have cared for People of Vision with a devotion similar to the nurturing I gave to my other four children.

For a while it became increasingly difficult to get experienced leadership in so many not-for-profit groups. Many women were using the skills they had perfected in charitable organizations to make money working in the business world. Still, I can't imagine that I would have worked nearly as hard at a paid job as I did in this community work, because I put my heart and soul and personal reputation into it.

Our daughter Marianne became active on the board of Prevent Blindness Indiana, then served as president of People of Vision. At this writing she is board president of Prevent Blindness Indiana. Seeing her and others of her generation accepting volunteer positions has given me a whole new perspective on the community contributions of young women of Marianne's generation. I find that although they are working at well-paid jobs or managing their own businesses, they do find time to give meaningful direction to Prevent Blindness. Their ability to network, calling on their friends by fax, e-mail, or cell phone for assistance in volunteer causes is impressive. I have witnessed volunteering come full circle with these well-organized and efficient young women as they network in People of Vision just as they network in their businesses. Like me, these women of a new generation find community service rewarding.

In celebration of POV's silver anniversary in 2005, I inaugurated life memberships for those who contributed a one-time gift of $1,000. This money is placed in an endowment to benefit Prevent Blindness Indiana. Our goal is to build this endowment to $100,000 by the end of 2007. Before the end of October 2007, our life membership list had already grown to eighty generous donors. I feel certain we will have one hundred life members before the fiscal year ends on March 31, 2008. Next I will be helping to insure the future stability of Prevent Blindness Indiana. Underlying funding for the future is important to sustain the life of a charitable organization, so we are now focusing on endowment-building as a part of our strategy. I plan to continue working for the prevention of blindness in the coming years.

Some interesting assignments as well as some recognition have come to me for my work in our community. In 1989 Governor Evan Bayh appointed me to serve for eight years on the Indiana Arts Commission. While enjoying various roles on this commission, I had the opportunity to see how other communities throughout the state were interacting with young Hoosiers as they participated in a wide variety of arts programs. At Union Station in October 2003, Gene and I jointly received the Indiana Governor's Arts Award.

Another honor Gene and I shared came in August 2007 from the Foundation Fighting Blindness in appreciation of our contribution to the Indiana University Medical Center. This gift provides funds to build the Eye Institute and create an endowment to insure that top researchers will be brought to the IUPUI campus. I believe it is possible that some of these scientists will be the ones to discover the breakthroughs so urgently needed to prevent blindness.

More recently, in September 2007, public broadcasting television station WFYI, at their tenth annual "Speaking of Women's Health" luncheon, honored Marianne and me for our philanthropy. And on November 8 2007, I received the Thomas Hasbrook Award from Bosma Enterprises for my concern for the blind and for saving sight. Shortly after I received notice of this award, I visited Bosma, a non-profit organization dedicated to assisting people with low vision or no vision in finding meaningful employment. At Bosma participants are trained to manage large departments in a packaging business which sends medical supplies all over the world. I was impressed with how well this business is managed and how professionally the managers interact with their employees. Additionally, Bosma has an outstanding daycare program for training the recently sight-impaired. Those in this program are taught Braille and other skills to get along with confidence in spite of their disabilities. I am aware that these awards convey not only individual recognition but also represent the work of many volunteers who have worked with me in service to the causes I have helped over the last sixty years.

During the 1990s the Eugene and Marilyn Glick Foundation increasingly became a vehicle for us to channel funds to philanthropic causes of interest to us in the Indianapolis community. For the most part, I did not take an active part in our foundation until recently. As we have grown older, I feel it is important for me to be more involved. I want to participate as we define our giving limits and direct the structure of our major contributions. Lately I have become considerably more active as we make these decisions.

Appropriate giving requires concentrated attention and diligent work. We want to be certain that the causes we support do improve life in this community and that the major gifts are going to the causes in which we are most interested. When Gene was working at Peoples State Bank in the forties, a young veteran of World War II did not have the money for a down payment on his first home. This young man's uncle came to the bank with him to provide the money. As the young man gratefully thanked his uncle, the older man told him, "Son, it is easy to give money away, but it is difficult to give it away intelligently."

That man's statement impressed Gene tremendously. And let me tell you it is a lot of hard work to be sure we give this money away intelligently. The foundation has recently begun stating its giving philosophy so its perameters are clear to the public. The Glick Foundation focus has been, and will be, limited to projects that might not otherwise happen. The focus of the foundation is aiding underprivileged children, low-income families, elderly citizens in our city, culture and the arts, medical and Jewish causes and nutrition and health. The foundation is interested in aiding start-up and unique projects, sponsoring incentive funding through matching grants and grants that will receive funding from additional sources. We will be best able to serve our community and our own family's intents if we limit ourselves to gifts in which we have had a sincere interest. We are unable to fund projects in which we have had no interest in our lifetime.

We also like to feel we are getting the most "bang for the buck," that is, the money we contribute does the most good for the most people.

Indianapolis has been very good to us, and it is only right that we should give back to this community and to the state of Indiana.

One of the most gratifying parts of our hard work with the foundation has been seeing the results of certain long-term projects. PRO-100 has been in existence for over twenty-five years. Juan Gant, Dean of Students at Broad Ripple High School, who serves as its director, has been involved in PRO-100 since its inception in 1982. He succeeded Dan Gallagher, who was PRO-100's first director, and also followed Dan in the dean's position at Broad Ripple

Now we can see the full benefits of that early program with successful graduates placed in important businesses and professions all over America. A young woman named Kimberly McElroy Jones recently wrote of her appreciation for the program, and we were pleased to meet her and learn more of her accomplishments.

Kimberly McElroy was in the second group of PRO-100 students in the early eighties. She received a BS in 2001, an MS in 2004, and is currently working on a PhD. Her current position is as Executive Director of the Metropolitan Indianapolis, Central Indiana Area Health Education Center, with her job involving the recruiting of minority young people for the health care industry in our city area.

Here is what she says about PRO-100 in a letter addressed to Gene:

> *You do not personally know me, but you have impacted my life greatly. When I was a teenaged girl you created a program called PRO-100. My mother was on public assistance and so I was considered a disadvantaged youth. As a result of this program, I was able to work on a golf course, earn money during the summer and gain a foundation for where I am today. One day you even took the time out to visit us and I was one of the fortunate youth who got to ride in your personal helicopter. . . .I want you to know that your generosity [has] not gone unnoticed and the impact on my life by people like yourself has been immeasurable. Thank you for recognizing the potential that is within all people, even those who grow up in environments which are not the best.*

Kimberly has recently undertaken a partnership with the Gene Glick Junior Achievement Center on Keystone Avenue near Glendale to set up a wellness clinic in their "Biz Town."

This brings us to the pride I feel for Junior Achievement, which the foundation has supported for years. Although I did not have an active part in planning the foundation's contribution to this center, I became most interested in its program: bringing schoolchildren from central Indiana schools to the large and well-appointed center, complete with a pizza parlor.

After six weeks of preparation in their classrooms, these groups of fifth grade children assume roles as business people in a make-believe town that replicates a real, thriving economy.

These are only a few of the many causes in the Indianapolis area which the foundation now supports.

And After PRO-100? Where did they go?

• Maurice Williams (PRO-100 1995) graduated from Purdue, received his law degree at IU, was president of the student law association and recently took a job in Washington D.C., as a U.S. patent attorney, his dream for many years.

• Robert Wilkins currently owns a tax service. During the slow times he does substitute teaching and he's also a coach in PRO-100.

• Duane Turner found himself attending West Point, but it was a different story not long ago. His hard-working family was below the poverty line like all the families in PRO-100, so the opportunity the program offered gave him experience he would use later in his life—to succeed.

These are only a few of the stories of the young people in this admirable "jump start" program.

For over ten years the Children's Bureau has worked closely with our foundation on the PRO-100 program. Several years ago we provided funds for expansion of the Homes for Black Children program at 38th and Tacoma, now known as the Fay Biccard Glick Family Place. A space within this building is designated as the Edith Shelton Wing. In May we provided funds at 71st and Michigan Road for the Fay Biccard Glick Neighorhood Center and the Fay Biccard Glick Family Pavilion. These facilities provide social and human services to children and families in need in a highly diversified community.

An example of our efforts to guide needy youngsters towards a promising future is our recent gift to the Children's Bureau Family Support Center. This center is the only children's shelter of its kind in Indiana. The services of the facility at Sixteenth Street and Martin Luther King, Jr. Boulevard are unique. The mission is to keep children out of the child welfare system by working with the entire family to strengthen parenting skills and to provide access to counseling and other services. In addition to housing a daycare for pre-school and foster-care children, this shelter provides emergency and respite care for abused and neglected children along with runaway and homeless youth. The building in which the Family Support Center has been operating is old and the space totally inadequate to accommodate the needs of these people.

We have made a challenge gift, matching dollar for dollar, up to $4 million to jump-start a campaign to fund construction of a new forty thousand-square-foot center at the present location. Being an adopted child myself, I know the importance of a stable, loving family. Gene and I believe in the Family Support Center's goal to be accessible to families who need help, to give them a place where they can feel welcome and comfortable, where they are treated with dignity and respect. Helping our most vulnerable children and families will only make our community a stronger and more desirable place in which to live.

For years Gene has been bothered by all the monuments and buildings we have in our city glorifying war. Of course he realizes honoring veterans has a place in our city; he is a veteran of World War II himself. But he has had a dream of erecting contemporary monuments to honor luminaries of the past two hundred years. The people he wished to honor were people of peace, whose creativity, intelligence, or concern for others have improved life for all mankind and have made this country great. But for years Gene's dream remained warm on the back burner.

I often wondered how such a goal might be accomplished, realizing that it would be an overwhelming project to honor these luminaries who have blessed humanity. I did not see how we could possibly do it.

So, when we were asked to contribute a lead gift to proceed with plans for the Cultural Trail, we were interested. It seemed to be a perfect fit for the dream both Gene and I had been nurturing for so long. The city of Indianapolis was planning to build a trail, with paths for pedestrians and bicycles. Along this trail, stretching from the heart of downtown Indianapolis for seven miles, will be displays of public art. The Cultural Trail will wander throughout the city to various areas of historical and cultural interest, from art galleries on Massachusetts Avenue to venues in Fountain Square. Plans call for it to extend past the Central Canal and Military Park all the way to Herron School of Art on the IUPUI campus. It will connect to the existing Monon Trail, which passes the Arts Park in

Broad Ripple and on out through Carmel.

We began meeting with Brian Payne of the Central Indiana Community Foundation and the architects hired to design the trail. It was decided to incorporate some of the monuments Gene had envisioned to beautify the trail and to inspire the visitors traveling along its way, honoring luminaries who have made this a better world for all mankind. In addition to the gift of $15 million for the trail, our foundation is also funding all of the architectural and construction expenses for the twelve sculptures honoring the luminaries.

We have had the plans approved by the city, and construction began in April 2007. In addition to a few of our sculptures in the center of downtown, we hope to have a concentration of ten luminaries within the span of a few blocks along the trail. Gene's concept is unique. We hope this will help our home city to grow as a tourist attraction, bringing people from all over the world to Indianapolis to see this Cultural Trail and to observe some of the outstanding contributing visionaries who have helped make this country great.

Over a period of months and through serious deliberations with those most interested in our foundation, including our daughters living in Indianapolis, we narrowed the twelve luminaries to these very special benefactors to humanity: Susan B. Anthony; Andrew Carnegie; Thomas Edison; Albert Einstein; Benjamin Franklin; Martin Luther King, Jr.; Abraham Lincoln; Franklin and Eleanor Roosevelt; Jonas Salk; Mark Twain; Booker T. Washington; and the Wright Brothers.

Our most recent contribution was the lead gift for an interactive center at the Indiana Historical society. This gift is significant because Gene and I feel strongly about preserving our family history. In 1997 Gene completed his autobiography, the book *Born to Build*. What prompted this book was his regret at not having asked his grandmother, Rachel Faust Glick, what her life was like when she was a little girl. The Civil War broke out when she was only six years old. Unfortunately, Rachel died when Gene was only ten, and he had never even thought of asking her to share her memories of the time when she was a child.

For many years Gene and I thought of writing a joint autobiography of our lives together. But when he began working on his autobiography, the emphasis was on the fiftieth anniversary of the Gene B. Glick Company. He wished to use his book as a primer for a successful life in business and an incentive for young people to become entrepreneurs. However, I never gave up on wanting to leave my history for my descendants because I believe it is extremely important for the younger generation to know about their ancestors.

Preserving history in a way that is appealing to youngsters is challenging today. Textbooks do not come to life, and pictures on the wall do not make significant impressions on most young minds these days. We are helping to fund an expansion to the History Center which will be known as The Indiana Experience. The new facility will not host traditional exhibits common in many museums. As director John Herbst explains it, "People will have experiences rather than look at artifacts." It will include computerized three-dimensional sets where visitors can "step into" the history of specific places and themes in Indiana history. One section will be entitled "Anything Goes." Here a recreated 1940s nightclub will feature the music of Cole Porter. In another area visitors can experience a hands-on conservation lab, restoring reproductions of historical documents and researching their family genealogy. The entire interactive project is unique, and we especially favor supporting projects that will benefit a large number of people.

Gene and I are fortunate to be able to serve and to give back to this community that has provided the opportunities for our financial success. To date the most significant contribution in the history of our foundation is our recent gift for the Eugene and Marilyn Glick Eye Institute at Indiana University School of Medicine. This is not only our largest gift, it is the culmination of more than a quarter of a lifetime devoted to the prevention of blindness.

Our gift for the Eye Institute provides funds for the building. It will also create an endowment with the hope that other generous donors will continue to support the research needed for major breakthroughs. Perhaps the cures we envision will one day come out of this facility at the Indiana University Medical Center. After all, it was scientists at IU who discovered the double helix. We are pleased and encouraged to learn the new president of Indiana University, Michael McRobbie, places life sciences at the top of his list to expand education and research. He intends to bring top faculty—Nobel laureates, Pulitzer Prize winners, and members of the National Academies and the American Academy of Arts and Sciences to teach at IU. My dream is for miracles to occur at this new institute.

...rs. Eugene B. Glick plays a game with her grandson, ...el Grande, 2½, asking him to indicate which way the E ...as she prepares to give him a home eye test.

In the second step of the test for vision problems in preschoolers, Mrs. Glick posts an E chart on a plain background at eye level 10 feet away from her grandson.

Here we are at a formal party in the lobby of the Circle theatre honoring supporters of the Indianapolis Symphony Orchestra. We have had symphony tickets for over sixty years.

PRO-100 1983 Riverside Crew October 11, 1983

(ftr) Andrea Chifton, Kimberly McElroy, Linda Bullock, Joseph Lee, Latrice Turnley, Lisa Holland. (br) Marcus Stennis, Tracy Goliday, James Gamble, Cletus D. Morris, supervisor.

Kimberly (McElroy) Jones, a proud graduate of PRO-100, with her husband, Reuben Jones.

Marianne was with me at the podium when we received an award for philanthropy from WFYI in 2007.

Gene came up with a charitable idea—to mark our fiftieth anniversary with a gala at the Indianapolis Museum of Art. Throughout the evening fifty guests' names were drawn to receive a $1,000 gift to their favorite charities from our foundation. All guests received a copy of Gene's autobiography Born to Build *that night.*

I was honored at the Prevention of Blindness Eye Ball when People of Vision celebrated their Silver Anniversary. I'm surrounded by past presidents (l-r) Sandy Obremsky, Helen Whipple, Marlene Hatch, Anne Schuster, Sheryl Babladelis, (Marilyn Glick,) Margaret Riser, Janet Barb, Carole Wainscott, Maxie Schnicke, Jackie Kalsbeck, Anne McDaniel and Jan Krukemeier.

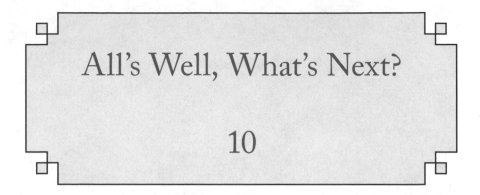

All's Well, What's Next?

10

More and more as the century drew to a close and moved on past the millennium, we focused our attention on our family. We took another trip to Europe in 1995. Gene wanted to show our children and older grandchildren the areas where he had fought in World War II. Gene and I traveled with Marianne, Arlene, Tom, Jackie, Mike, Brian, Lynda, Mark, Alice, and Andrew. We went first to London, where we saw the sights and traveled through the newly opened "Chunnel" beneath the English Channel to France. Then we met our guide for the trip to see Gene's war sites.

Gene's former business associate and longtime consultant Lou Palma had researched areas where Gene's regiment, the Thunderbirds, had fought during the war, so we journeyed on to the sites of fighting in the Alsace-Lorraine area. It was so peaceful when we stopped to reflect by the Mozelle River. As we sat in these beautiful surroundings, Gene spoke to us about what it was like for him to cross that river under fire on his first day at the front. Our family had not heard this story because Gene never dwelt on the hardships he had endured in the war. Few of his regiment survived. Glick (*gleück*) means "luck" in German, and Gene was lucky to come home unscathed.

In a small town near Épinal, our guide stopped at the mayor's office as we passed. Out came the mayor, who looked like Jiggs, a comic character popular in the "funny papers" when Gene and I were kids. This mayor had fought with the Thunderbirds and felt a kinship with us. He ran over to his house around the corner and brought back not only refreshments, but his lifelong pal, who had also fought with Gene's regiment.

The mayor asked Gene to send him the patch the Thunderbirds wore on their uniforms. Later that summer Gene obliged.

We stopped at the beautiful, but sad, American cemetery nearby, where so many of the markers identified boys who had fought with Gene's group. Then we moved on into Germany, where we were able to spend time once more at the cemeteries in Alsdorf and Gailingen, so more of the family could see the resting places of their ancestors.

When we reached Munich, we made a point of visiting Dachau. Gene was among the first of the American troops to liberate Dachau, and it was photos of this concentration camp that Gene had been showing family friends early in August 1945, when I first visited his home. Now, on our 1995 tour, we observed that Dachau was cleaned up and sterilized, with its bunk beds, strangely, looking like those at a summer camp for children. It is impossible to recapture the awful things that went on there from the displays and movies visitors see before entering the area where inmates were quartered, but we were glad we visited.

Gene most of all enjoyed eating sauerbraten in Rottenberg, and from there we drove to Salzburg in Austria and on into Italy, where Gene had spent some months in a replacement depot in 1944 before heading on to active duty in France.

This trip with the children and grandchildren made me appreciate how good it was to be living in the United States of America.

Back home we continued our custom begun in the 1990s of going out to dinner almost every evening of the week with the most interesting people: civic and political leaders and those in the performing arts. It enables us to keep up with Indianapolis affairs and to share conversation with a variety of friends and acquaintances. Some of the people are development directors for charities, "developing" us. Gene says, "They want to separate us from our money."

When we dined at home, our meals were prepared by our cook, Edith Shelton, a talented woman sent to me in 1971 by the Indiana State Employment agency. Edith stayed with us for almost thirty years.

There were others before Edith, and they became part of the family, too. Since they were so close to us, their lives are worthy of mention.

When Alice was born, wishing to have a baby nurse for at least a few weeks, I hired Mrs. Terwilliger to take care of the new baby. When I first called her, I asked if she would consider staying with us for several months. She declined. However, when she had been in the house for a week or so, she said, "Mrs. Glick, would you still like for me to stay on with you?" She stayed for seven years, doing everything, including cleaning, cooking, laundry, and childcare.

Not long after we moved into the new house, Mrs. Terwilliger retired. Our girls had flourished under her care and we all missed her. The following spring at Easter time, I invited her to come back and fly down with us to Florida to take care of eighteen-month-old Lynda. They stayed with a family we knew well, close to the Yacht Club in West Palm Beach, while the rest of us were not far away on the ocean. When I went to see Lynda, she was so preoccupied playing with a kitten that she didn't even look up at me to say goodbye—a testament to her contentment with Mrs. Terwilliger.

In February 1960 I hired Mae Virginia Baker as housekeeper and laundress, and she was with us for nineteen years. When she began drawing her Social Security, she left us, but we stayed in touch, and for years she came to visit us right after Thanksgiving week each year. Several years ago Gene and I joined her large family at the Iron Skillet to celebrate her ninetieth birthday.

Now I must tell you about our beloved cook Edith, who cooked so many delicious meals. We shared a family relationship and literally cared for each other.

When I interviewed Edith in 1971 and wanted references, she provided the name of Ivan Tors, who made animal documentary films for a California studio. He was in Europe, and I chased him by phone through England, then Italy, where I finally reached him. His wife had been ill and Edith had taken care of the children, cooked, did all the housework, and drove the Tors children to school. He gave Edith an A+ reference.

Edith arrived at our home the day we moved back into the reconstructed house after the fire. We worked together side by side unwrapping and washing all the new dishes and other items from the move. I was certain this woman was a gem. When she failed to return the next day, I was shocked and asked Virginia what she thought had happened. "You didn't pay her when she left yesterday," she said. Virginia explained to me that Edith had done only day work when she came to Indianapolis, and was insulted when I failed to pay her. I had assumed she was to be a permanent employee and receive her pay her at the end of the week. I immediately phoned Edith to explain and coaxed her to come back. Thankfully she did return to stay with us for almost thirty years. She was an outstanding cook for all our family meals. And she made a breeze of entertaining for cocktail parties, dinner parties, and charitable events.

Edith had her own bedroom and bath in our home, but she never spent the night unless we were out of town. Even if we returned as late as 3 o'clock in the morning, she went to her own home at Fifty-second and Winthrop, where she supervised a complicated family situation.

After Edith had a stroke in the late 1990s, she was able to work only part-time. Our children were grown, and we no longer needed a live-in cook. At that time I arranged for an exceptionally capable man, Herb Howard, to cook for us. Herb had retired from his long-time job in charge of catering at the Eli Lilly and Company home office downtown.

We had come to know Herb as a bartender at weekend parties in our own home and in the homes of friends. He began working with Edith, learning from her how to cook food the way we like it for our traditional Sabbath meals and subsequently for each Monday night as well. It was nice to have one dinner a week, just the two of us at home.

One Monday evening while Herb was preparing dinner, I began to tell him how the special Friday night dinner became a tradition for our family, as we all enjoyed being together to welcome the Sabbath each week. It stretched all the way back to the days when Gene and I were dating.

On Friday nights we went to temple services with the older ladies, then dropped them off at the Elks Club while we went dancing. When we lived in the house on Wallace, we ate together as quickly as we could. Then we hurried off, taking the two grandmothers to temple and leaving Marianne, Arlene, and Alice with the housekeeper. Because of Gene's late schedule at the building sites, we found we were arriving late for the services, and it was a mad dash. So we stopped going to temple after dinner each Friday. Instead, we had a leisurely meal with both grandmothers and the children. Since that time we have continued to enjoy very pleasant Sabbath evenings with our family.

This departure from decades of strong attachment to synagogue and temple did cause me some concern. You will recall that I was pious and observant as a young girl. I had come from Detroit, which has a very observant Jewish community. Conservative Judaism maintained many of the older traditions. It was this tradition that I observed after my father died, and I really believe it carried me through that difficult time. Every Saturday morning I was at services in the Junior Congregation.

When I was a young bride in Indianapolis, I might have joined both the Conservative and Reform temples, but because Gene had not had a Bar Mitzvah and would have been uncomfortable in a service conducted mostly in Hebrew, we joined the Indianapolis Hebrew Congregation, where his family was so deeply rooted.

However, our Reform congregation has changed. Following the national trend of Reform congregations, Indianapolis Hebrew Congregation in the 1970s began to adopt more traditional rituals. We now have more Hebrew in our prayer book, and our cantor Janet Roger has a beautiful voice that enriches our services tremendously. Unlike in our children's times, youngsters now study to become a Bar (masculine) or Bat (feminine) Mitzvah, which increases their Hebrew literacy.

When I have been able to attend Friday night services at IHC these days, I have found that they are quite upbeat. In some ways I feel we are missing something by omitting these services each week, but I love our family tradition. It is still impossible for us to have an early dinner and attend temple services at the same time. We have made accommodations for our children and little great-grandchildren. Now that our company is no longer engaged in construction, Gene is home early on Friday evening, so we can have our great-grandchildren at the Sabbath table.

Marianne and her husband will usually be with us on Friday nights. She is happily married to Mike Woods, for which Gene and I are grateful. Marianne and Mike were good friends for many years before they married, and it's obvious they truly enjoy, accept, and encourage one another. In the fall of 2004 Marianne decided she'd like to try her hand at painting and began taking drawing lessons at North Central High School. Later she took classes at the Indianapolis Art Center. Now she travels wherever noted artists are offering special workshops. She has become passionate about her art and was gratified to have her watercolors selected for juried shows of the Watercolor Society of Indiana, the Pasadena Learning & Art Expo, and the Midwest National Abstract Exhibition. Her work has also been exhibited at the Indianapolis Art Center, the Sullivan-Munce Cultural Center, Eagle Creek Coffee Company in Zionsville, and at Art House, sponsored by *Indianapolis Monthly* magazine. She has a website and is selling her watercolor and acrylic creations through the internet.

Marianne is a past president of People of Vision and current president of Prevent Blindness Indiana. In 2006 she was appointed by Governor Mitch Daniels to Ball State University's trustees. She also serves on the boards of a number of other major civic organizations throughout our city. Besides the volunteering and painting she enjoys biking, power-walking, gardening, entertaining, and family responsibilities.

Arlene and her husband Tom Grande often join us with their oldest daughter Jackie and her husband, Dave Barrett. Jackie and Dave are the parents of Joel, seven years old at this writing, and Allison, age five. The baby Jessica is now two and quite the young lady. In September 2007 the Temple Sisterhood asked Jackie if she, her daughters, mother, and grandma (me) would model together at the fall luncheon, as a four-generation family. Jessica loved presenting herself and was extremely unhappy when she had to leave the stage.

Besides Jackie, Arlene and Tom have four other children, including Mike, with UBS Financial in Chicago, and Brian, who joined the Glick Company in November 2007.

Laura, Arlene and Tom's youngest daughter, has completed her junior year at the University of Dayton in Ohio. She wants to be an art teacher. She has recently served as a summer intern at the Children's Museum in Chicago. Their youngest, Ben, is a junior at Brebeuf, where he's a star on the hockey team.

Arlene enjoys attending services at the temple and participates in a number of activities there. She has served on the board of Hadassah, in which she has a devoted interest. She and Tom have been the most enthusiastic supporters of their children's athletic activities, attending all the games in which their children participated. Forty hours after Laura was born, I recall, Arlene was at Michael's soccer game. So Gene and I met them at the game with a lunch we picked up at Shapiro's deli. Then, after a hurried lunch, we took the new baby and went to Brian's baseball game.

Arlene and Tom remain avid golfers. At Broadmoor Country Club Arlene won the ladies eighteen-hole golf championship five times. A few years ago the Grandes left Broadmoor, a thirty-five-minute drive from their home in Carmel. They joined Bridgewater, ten minutes away, where they fell in love with the course and the clubhouse, then noticed a lot there right on the golf course which seemed to "fit them like a glove," so they bought it, built on it, and moved into their beautiful new home.

We always see Alice in Florida. Alice and Andrew's daughter Karyn, an academic whiz just like her mother, has finished her junior year at the University of Miami in Coral Gables. She has a scholarship covering 75% of tuition. Karyn presently is serving as senior news editor of the college newspaper. In the summer of '07 she traveled to Shanghai for six weeks with a group from the college newspaper who were writing articles for publication after the group's return. Their older daughter, Dora, has been promoted to manager of East West Books, a health food store in Brooklyn. Alice tells me Dora recently created a new healthy cocktail that is selling very well. Business has increased under Dora's supervision. Is it possible that her aptitude for business may be more profitable than her artistic talent, and she may reserve her art work for leisure time?

Each fall we take a trip to California to spend time with Lynda and her husband Mark. Their daughter Lauren (whom Gene nicknamed Gigi) has returned to the University of Southern California in Santa Barbara for her sophomore year. She works at a golf course during the summers to earn her own spending money. Her brother Jonathan attends Indiana University in Bloomington and has joined the ZBT fraternity. Jonathan spends some weekends with us in Indianapolis. We expect him to go on to graduate school after he gets his BS degree from the Kelley School of Business.

Having Jonathan at the house is delightful, but a little unusual for us. I never was a baby-sitting grandmother. When Arlene married young and had children right away, I was leading a very active life of my own with Lynda still at home. I didn't make myself available for staying with Arlene's little ones, and that has not changed. We see Jackie's children frequently, and I especially appreciate having them around our family table on Sabbath and the High Holy Days.

Several years ago Herb Howard fell down a flight of stairs in his home and is no longer able to work. Since that time I have engaged a caterer to prepare our family dinners, which are "heart healthy" and prepared Pritikin style.

Gene and I eat very little meat in accordance with the Pritikin diet, which emphasizes complex carbohydrates, whole grains, vegetables and fruit. We continue to enjoy excellent health. After spending two weeks in the Pritikin program at their centers each October from 1987 through 2000, fourteen straight years, I can credit the Pritikin program for our well-being. Obesity would not be the problem it is today if everyone's diet was based on the Pritikin food pyramid.

I became interested in Pritikin because of Dorothy Gerson, who had been going to Pritikin since the late 1970s. On visits to the Pritikin Center in California, the Gersons became well acquainted with Nathan Pritikin. This founder of the program had a doctorate in physics, not medicine.

Dorothy encouraged me to read his book, and later I became a believer.

We sent Edith to Pritikin in the hopes she could lose weight, and although she didn't stay with the program, I decided to go myself.

While at Pritikin, participants are offered so many interesting experiences each day that being there is truly a learning experience and a lot of fun. There are daily cooking classes and fitness training throughout the day with a variety of equipment. Yoga, pilates, and water exercises are optional. One evening each month they take a group to a grocery store to experience heart-healthy shopping. But all participants benefit from scheduled lectures by dieticians, nutritionists, psychologists, and other experts. These talks are designed to help develop good habits for a healthier lifestyle. Dr. Nathan Pritikin lectured every session while he was alive; now his son Robert, a medical doctor, continues the tradition. All participants at Pritikin must take a stress test before they are allowed to use the exercise equipment, and they have blood check-ups and sessions with the doctors at the facility throughout their visit.

Pritikin was not the only program that has helped keep us healthy. After Gene read an article in *Executive Health* magazine about the diagnostic clinic at the magnificent Greenbrier Resort Hotel in the mountains, we made our first visit in October 1962. We have had all of our complete physical examinations at the Greenbrier every year since that time, until 2007.

The extensive physical exam regime at the Greenbrier is a bit like an assembly line. The day begins about 7:30 a.m. with a visit to the doctor, who at the end of the first exam writes out the tests to be completed. First stop is the lab, from there to the nurses' station, and then to X-ray. A second blood test takes place at the lab two hours after breakfast. All of the test equipment is right there and state-of-the-art. The entire physical is usually completed by noon. If the doctor wants an additional test, perhaps a colonoscopy, a stress test, or a sonogram, these procedures are available the next day in the clinic. A final meeting with the doctor for a review of the test results completes the exam. Patients are usually finished by noon and can play golf or engage in other activities for the rest of the day.

This year we decided we ought to have an internist at home and have arranged with Dr. Greg Gramelspacher of the Indiana University Medical Center to be our physician. Now we can have our annual physicals close to home. The summer of 2007 was the first time we did not have our exams at the Greenbrier.

It was 1962 when the Greenbrier doctor advised me to watch the nodule on my neck, which I mentioned earlier. After a series of tests in Indianapolis, the module was removed to check for a possible malignancy. Fortunately it was benign, and I was blessed to live on with my family for so many more years.

One of the things we are continually grateful for is our family home. Its beauty has been enhanced throughout the years. Twenty years ago Gene wanted to install a big screen TV so that he could practice his golf swing while watching two monitors. On one monitor he planned to watch a tape of Jack Nicklaus, while on the other he could record his own swing as he attempted to swing like the pro. With this inspiration, we agreed to add one thousand square feet to the northwest side of our home. Without all this additional room, I could never have amassed several hundred pieces of contemporary studio glass sculptures.

Gene and I have formally assigned 90% of the glass collection to the Indianapolis Museum of Art. Still, much of the collection remains with us, gracing every corner of our home. Art study groups come to learn about the glass, and I like telling them all about the artists and my experiences collecting this magical work.

We have enjoyed the extended space tremendously. For a long time Gene used Styrofoam pellets as he practiced in the new great room, but he never did come close to swinging like any of the professionals he so painstakingly tried to emulate.

Now, as my golf game has deteriorated, I try to console myself by observing not even Jack Nicklaus nor Arnie Palmer can score today as well as they did before they were fifty plus years old. When we were young and played a lot of golf along with many hours of practice, our golf did improve.

Today we still go out to Crooked Stick or Broadmoor, where we can enjoy the beauty of the golf course. We are just glad to be together, and we do the best we can. It is truly a lot more fun if we take the bad shots over and do not even bother to keep score.

There is a proverb that teaches us to pray that we may be able to "change the things that can be changed, accept the things that cannot be changed, and have the wisdom to know the difference."

Now Gene and I are in our eighth decades and still full of energy and enthusiasm for life. At this age, as I am writing this story for family and friends, I find it gratifying to look back on my journey through life.

Over the years perceptions change, and experiences seem a little different from what they once appeared to be. I have learned a lot and appreciate the new insights.

Gene and the children have been first and foremost in my life. As I look back at those days when the children were young, I realize I worried about being a good mother for years. Perhaps others feel this way too, but I think my insecurities as a young woman made me sensitive to my inadequacies. I was so inexperienced, and I had no background for mothering.

Those early years with the children were difficult for me. My idea of motherhood was what I'd seen in the movies. When babies cried, they were given a bottle, then cooed or smiled and played or went to sleep looking like little angels. My first three girls were born within three years and eight months, and sometimes they were angels but more often they were normally active, and at times even frustrating, uncooperative little imps.

I had grown up in a very orderly, peaceful household. There were many undercurrents, but it was quiet. Now I experienced crying, fighting, spilling—in short, constant chaos—and I was completely overwhelmed. The only time it was quiet was when they all watched television. They sat down on small stools before *Ding Dong School* with Miss Frances Horowitz each morning. At the end of the program she advised the children, "Call Mummy," and I came to listen to her promotion for Gerber's baby food. At the end of this commercial, she sported a big, benevolent smile and said, "Have FUN with your children." Well, I wasn't having any fun, and the tears would stream down my face because she implied I should be having fun like all those other mothers out there in TV land. I was a failure at this most important job of my life.

And yet I was trying to do a good job, involving them in many activities, encouraging them, listening to them, attending to their needs. My children were caring for each other and loving Gene and me, and they were succeeding in school. Still, for many years I did not believe I was an adequate mother. Now that I see how well they have grown up, how they care for their families and others, I realize that I did do a good job. Long ago I came to terms with those negative feelings, but they were ever so disturbing at the time.

Looking back on it now, I can how the difficulties with my mother continued to bother me as long as she was alive. No wonder I had difficulty trying to cope with my own children.

There is no good reason for rehashing the past unless it brings constructive action for the present and future. So these reflections have great value and have helped me understand some things that baffled me in the past. One thing I want my descendants to learn from this story is to expect challenges as they travel through life. When they face their difficulties with a positive attitude, they will win their battles.

And to my contemporaries I recommend that they take the time to review their lives and reveal to their descendants, whether on a tape recorder or by written words, the stories they remember and what has had meaning for them. It is time-consuming but so very rewarding. Those who take this advice will surely be glad they did.

Through the process of reviewing my life I have gained insights about my mother and her relationship to me. Even though my mother was neurotic, while my father was living I had ten good years of her loving attention and meticulous care. Then, everything changed after my father died. She scolded me without mercy, and all I was able to do was cry. The pain of losing her approval was just too deep and overwhelming. I was not aware of how angry I was. The tears came so quickly that I was unable to voice my anger.

The challenges increased after we moved to Indianapolis and I had acquired many new friends. She chided me then about them: I was staying home too much and ignoring them or I was out too much and ignoring her. Neither she nor I recognized all of her constant reprimanding reflected her own misery within; she must have felt her unhappiness was my fault. Years later I learned people tend to blame others for their own shortcomings. Surely my mother must have loved me to the best of her ability when I was no longer a little child. I never appreciated her loving care over all the years until recently, while working on this book.

The ambivalence I felt for her had bothered me for years, and now I am able to sympathize with her plight and appreciate her concerns, the love she did give me, and all she did to make me a better person than I might have been. She certainly challenged me, and though I hated it at the time, I think it made me strong.

Today I am glad that I am no longer burdened by the resentment and ambivalence these early experiences created. And I guess I was born with an optimistic nature. After most confrontations with my mother, she'd go visit a neighbor and I'd wipe my tears away, put on some makeup, get dressed up attractively, and treat myself to a long walk up Meridian Street. I'd convince myself new possibilities were surely on the horizon and life was good.

Partly I think I survived because when life gave me "flight or fight" options, I was not one to flee. All the time I was growing up, as I was struggling to overcome difficulties, smiling and acting submissive to retain the love of the only person who could take care of me, I must have been sublimating a very dominant spirit. Inside me was a mighty will to survive.

I've thought about the effects of heredity and environment and how these two factors shape one's life. I had a very good environment when I was a young child. But my sister Frances grew up in a poor environment. Our father, Isidore Ornstein, was irresponsible, moving his family around Coney Island, neglecting to pay his rent. He must have been evicted frequently. That is why the adoption authorities could not find him.

Frances's stepmother Bessie didn't speak English, she cooked greasy Eastern European-style food, and this woman and my father wouldn't permit Frances go to the school that wanted to give her a scholarship. In another of those interesting parallels between my life and Frances's, my mother, Rose Koffman, once told the social worker visiting her to explain about a college scholarship for me that she did not want me to go to college. She wanted me to get a job.

My sister became bitter toward her father, and yet she too persevered, married, and successfully raised two children, while still experiencing tragedy when her two babies died. And she handled her cancer heroically.

Both my sister and I had the good fortune and sense of direction to find success and happiness. This is an argument for heredity. Our mother, who died when I was born, had to have had a strong personality and must have been the strength of the small Ornstein family.

Maybe I was motivated by the Koffmans, or perhaps I was born to be strong and to get the knowledge I needed to be what some call a "quick study." Throughout my teens and into my twenties, I seemed to know how to take advantage of opportunities and to improve whatever tasks came my way.

I sometimes wonder how much of what we do is programmed by our genes or by training and environment. I recall in the musical *South Pacific* there is a scene where the American soldier sings to his Asian lover, "You have to be carefully taught to hate all the people your relatives hate." We learn so much at home early in life.

I tried to improve on my opportunities. I read Dale Carnegie and remembered what he said. And, as I was working for Indianapolis Life Insurance Company when I did not feel capable of answering specific letters, I'd take them to the head of the department to help me solve the problem. Apparently the other girls didn't have the initiative or instincts to do that, and they did not advance as I did. This paid off when an opportunity for promotion came along, I was asked to move up to the Reinsurance Department, where I later became head of that department and secretary to the vice president, Walter Huehl.

As a newcomer to Indianapolis, I enjoyed the challenge of being hospitality chairman for Temple Teens. I knew nothing about this task, but with good advice I learned quickly. I always welcomed new challenges.

Years later, when I began collecting studio glass, it was necessary for me to learn from the ground up. I asked the art museum's director for advice, and he told me, "Only buy good art." This was more challenging and did not happen quickly. Patience, persistence, and determination were required to learn as much as I could by studying art books and magazines and making personal visits to galleries and museums over a period of years.

Being able to seize opportunity is important, too. Opportunity may knock softly, but some never hear it. Then there is the role of chance or destiny. It is possible that some things that happen were meant to be, as if they are the will of God. From my own experience I surmise this is true.

That bridge game on December 5, 1945, when Gene and I first talked, was unbelievable. I know Gene had no desire to come to that game. And afterwards I didn't need much help putting away things from the bridge game, but I did want somebody to help me get the extra card table and chairs returned to the next-door neighbor. That gave us the opportunity to talk for two hours. All the rest, of course, "is history."

Instinct helps. I recognized in those two hours that Gene was a substantial fellow, and he had the character and moral values I had so admired in my father. It was not "love at first sight." I thought, "Here is the kind of boy I could marry." And one month later, on January 5, 1946, Gene proposed and I was ready. During the thirty-one days from December 5 until the night of January 5, we saw each other almost every day. We became close in thought and feeling as our mutual affection grew and we found happiness together. It did not occur to me that I was in love. It was almost Christmas when we shared our first kiss under the mistletoe at the

Elks Club. I do recall hoping he would kiss me before that time. And I remember while we kissed at midnight, January 1, 1946, I was wishing we would be together every New Year's Eve thereafter. On that night I am sure I loved him and hoped he would feel that way too some day. The following Friday night after dancing at the Sapphire Room we spent a long time talking in the car when he proposed. I was certainly willing but completely surprised that my wish had been granted so quickly.

Later, when I hired helpers I could tell instinctively who would be right. I made good choices and was fortunate to find people whom we came to regard as members of our family. They stayed with us for many years.

All through the years I have tried to avoid conflict. If I can go along without crossing people, that's the way I like it. When Gene wants to go to a certain restaurant, I just agree. What difference does it make? If I don't agree with his choice that evening, it isn't worth making a fuss. There are some things I feel strongly about, and I have ways of compromising and getting around the issues that are important to me.

I think I may have a diplomatic nature; otherwise when my parents' friends asked whether I liked my mother or father better, why did I say I liked them both the same? I was only three years old.

Friendships were always important to me, and I do think friends affect our development as we grow throughout our lives. Certainly my best friends in Detroit, June Smith, Rosalie Frank, Miriam Weisman, and especially Dorothy Davidson helped me grow. And later, when I came to Indianapolis, my closest friends Marjorie Rab and Annette Simon all influenced me as did the Deb-Ette club, the dances, the parties, all the dates that were fun and wholesome—lots of group dating. Today the dating situation is quite different.

In recent years I have had the opportunity to meet wonderful people, and I treasure these new friends. Still, I cherish the friends I have held dear over many years. They are always in my thoughts, and I try to let them know I care. There is a saying, "You can never do a kindness too soon, for you never know how soon it will be too late." Over the past few years these words of wisdom have eased our pain when long-time friends are suddenly gone. It has been comforting to know we acted before it was too late.

A special hero was Gil Bloch, a dear Florida friend, who suffered a debilitating illness which gradually destroyed his muscles over a period of fifteen years until he died. When we first met this brilliant, "macho" guy at High Ridge Country Club, he was a low handicap golfer. He was always entertaining, and that continued no matter how ill he became. While confined to his wheelchair, he courageously said, "In this life you have to play the hand you are dealt."

How true. I am not one to yearn for the past. This is the day, the moment we have, and let us all try to make the most of it. There are so many satisfactions in my life now, and I suppose there always have been.

I really don't have any important regrets. To tell the truth this Cinderella is totally content in her castle, grateful every day for all the treasures life has bestowed on her.

Captured at the moment: Gene and Marilyn congratulate Gordon St. Angelo in November, 2007, on his many years of service to the community. Gordon is the president and CEO of the Milton and Rose Friedman Foundation, which focuses on charter schools.

I love this photo of Lynda and Mark, Jonathan and Lauren when these children were young in the late eighties.

Jackie's children— Allison, Jessica and Joel in 2007.

In the early eighties we had fun dressing up at Mackinac Island to pose for this photo, with (l-r) Lynda, Mark, Marilyn, Gene, Marianne, Fritz Monson, Alice, Arlene, and Tom.

Marianne, Alice, Arlene, Barbara, Lynda.

Gil Bloch and his wife Bea were golfing partners in Palm Beach. They became more like close relatives, sharing family events in California, Indiana, and Florida.

My birthday party at Miriam Landman's home, March, 2007. Miriam (ft. l corner) and her daughter Nancy (ft. r corner) and family members who could be in Indy to celebrate.

From me and my "Prince of a Fellow"—CHEERS!

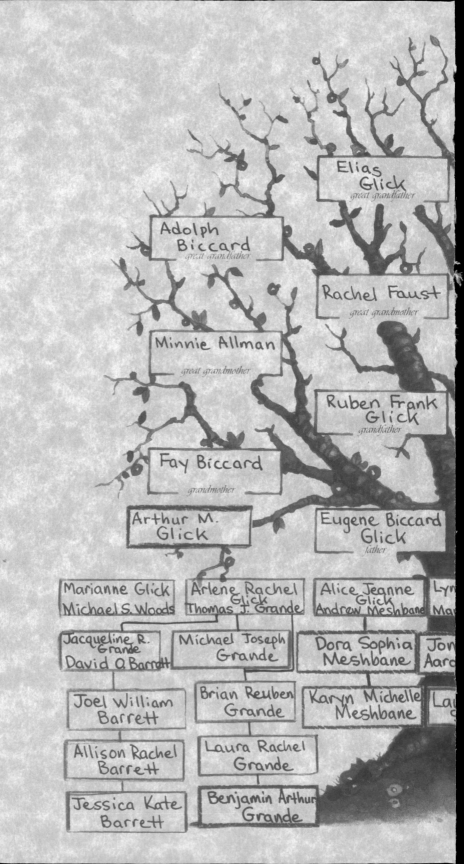

Elias Glick
great grandfather

Adolph Biccard
great grandfather

Rachel Faust
great grandmother

Minnie Allman
great grandmother

Ruben Frank Glick
grandfather

Fay Biccard
grandmother

Arthur M. Glick

Eugene Biccard Glick
father

Marianne Glick
Michael S. Woods

Arlene Rachel Glick
Thomas J. Grande

Alice Jeanne Glick
Andrew Meshbane

Lyn
Ma

Jacqueline R. Grande
David O. Barrett

Michael Joseph Grande

Dora Sophia Meshbane

Jon
Aaro

Joel William Barrett

Brian Reuben Grande

Karyn Michelle Meshbane

La

Allison Rachel Barrett

Laura Rachel Grande

Jessica Kate Barrett

Benjamin Arthur Grande